Voices
of the
Razorbacks

Voices
of the
Razorbacks

A history of Arkansas's
iconic sports broadcasters

Hoyt Purvis
and Stanley Sharp

The Butler Center for Arkansas Studies
Central Arkansas Library System
100 Rock Street
Little Rock, Arkansas 72201
www.butlercenter.org

First Printing: September 2013

ISBN 978-1-935106-62-3
e-ISBN 978-1-935106-63-0

Project director: Rod Lorenzen
Copyeditor: Ali Welky
Book and cover design: H. K. Stewart

Library of Congress Cataloging-in-Publication Data
Purvis, Hoyt H.
Voices of the Razorbacks / Hoyt Purvis, Stanley Sharp.
    pages cm
Summary: "The creation and development of the Razorback Sports Network not only helped to
build a loyal following for the Razorbacks, but also forged a close identification among
Razorback fans with broadcasters such as Paul Eells and Bud Campbell, who became "voices of
the Razorbacks." A sense of kinship developed within the audience, and the broadcasts of
Razorback sports have become an integral part of the state's culture"-- Provided by publisher.
ISBN 978-1-935106-62-3 (pbk.) -- ISBN 978-1-935106-63-0 (e-book)
1. Television broadcasting of sports--Arkansas--History. 2. University of Arkansas,
Fayetteville--Sports--History. I. Title.

GV742.3.P87 2013
796.332'630976714--dc23

2013018862

Printed in the United States of America
This book is printed on archival-quality paper that meets requirements of the
American National Standard for Information Sciences, Permanence of Paper,
Printed Library Materials, ANSI Z39.48-1984.

The publishing division of the Butler Center for Arkansas Studies
was made possible by the generosity of Dora Johnson Ragsdale and
John G. Ragsdale Jr.

To Mary and to Pamela and Camille for their support and for accompanying me to so many sports events over the years, and to Wells, Duke, Barrett, and Sienna, with the hope that sports will provide you with as much enjoyment as it has for me.

— HP

To my mother Jaquita Sharp and my two sons Peyten and Matthew Sharp for their love and support; to my fellow author Hoyt Purvis for guiding me through graduate school; and to the memory of my namesake, Stan "The Man" Musial.

— SCS

Contents

Acknowledgements...9

Introduction: Distinctive History and Role
    of Razorback Broadcasting...11

1. Beginnings: 1940s and '50s...17

2. 1960s and Frank Broyles Era..51

3. The Great Shootout and the 1970s: National Television 67

4. Into the 1980s and the Paul Eells Era 79

5. Into the 1990s: Mike Nail Steps In 95

6. Into a New Millennium: Chuck Barrett,
    Little Rock, and Fayetteville...111

7. Today's Razorback Broadcasting: A Booming Business 139

Conclusion: The Legacy 149

Index 151

About the Authors..163

Acknowledgements

Appreciation is due to many for their assistance with this book. It would be impossible to list all who helped in various ways, but special gratitude goes to Bob Cheyne, the late Bob Fulton, the late Charlie Jones, Mike Nail, Tommy Booras, Chuck Barrett, Rick Schaeffer, Grant Hall, Larry Foley, Gerald Jordan, Dennis Kirkpatrick, Kevin Trainor, Jim Borden, Randy Dixon, Steve Barnes, Mary Lynn Gibson, Marti Thomas, Carol Rachal, Scott Lunsford, Tim Nutt, Nate Allen, KATV, Special Collections–University of Arkansas Libraries, the David and Barbara Pryor Center for Arkansas Oral and Visual History, Dale Carpenter, and the Walter J. Lemke Department of Journalism, University of Arkansas.

Also, special thanks to Rod Lorenzen and Ali Welky of the Butler Center for Arkansas Studies and to H. K. Stewart.

While many have been helpful on this project, the authors are responsible for any mistakes or omissions.

Introduction: Distinctive History and Role of Razorback Broadcasting

The broadcasting of Arkansas Razorback sports at the University of Arkansas has a unique history. The original Razorback network established more than 60 years ago was a pioneering effort in collegiate sports broadcasting. The creation and development of the network helped to build not only interest in the Razorbacks and a loyal following for the teams, but also forged a close identification among Razorback fans with some of the broadcasters. The broadcasts of Razorback sports created a sense of kinship among the audience members and became an integral part of the state's culture.

There was a time when some owners of major league baseball teams opposed allowing their games to be broadcast because they believed that doing so would cut into ticket sales. Eventually, most came to the view that broadcasts could be an excellent promotional tool and help build interest, developing and sustaining what later would be known as a "fan base." Certainly, broadcasts of Arkansas sports, beginning with football, were major factors in developing devoted and enduring followers of the Razorbacks.

As Bob Cheyne—the University of Arkansas's first sports publicity director and a key figure in building the Razorback network—said, "Nothing contributed to the interest in Razorback football more than having a statewide network." Mike Nail, one of the major voices of the Razorbacks, said that the Arkansas network "continues to be a positive influence on the success and promotion of Razorback athletics."

In touting its broadcasts to stations and advertisers in 2007, Arkansas Razorback Sports Network (ARSN) put out this statement: "We challenge you to find another state or major market that can offer a captured audience on the scale that we can. When you combine these factors along with solid performance that our seasoned broadcast team delivers week after week, you get results for your clients." That statement illustrates the distinctiveness of Razorback sports broadcasting.

Veteran sports journalist Harry King remembers, "At one time, almost every radio station in the state subscribed to the network. That's how people got their Razorback coverage. It was either that or wait until the next day for the newspaper. You could never replace those days, because of TV and technology. It was not unusual then to have a family gathering—six or eight people—standing around a radio. And, if you were really lucky, somebody brought cheese dip."

Former coach and athletic director Frank Broyles, like John Barnhill before him, understood the importance of having Razorback broadcasts on the air around the state. Broyles said Barnhill's idea was a brilliant one and that giving broadcasting rights to stations all over the state was a huge factor in the success of Razorback sports. "Everyone in the state was listening to the Razorbacks. We developed a strong fan base. It's continued to grow into what it is today," Broyles told Kelly Kemp of *Celebrate Arkansas* magazine.

The number of radio stations carrying Razorback games has varied over the years, although there are fewer stations in the network in recent years than there once were. From the original 34 stations in 1951, the network steadily climbed to 80 stations by 1964 and nearly 100 by 1968. There were as many as 116 in 1976, and in 1994–95, the basketball network had 87 stations, including some that were combination AM-FM, and several in surrounding states. In more recent times, the network has averaged 50 to 60 stations. In 2008, there were 53 stations on the football network and 56 stations for basketball in 2008–09. The ARSN affiliate list for 2012–13 included 52 stations, blanketing Arkansas and parts of all six surrounding states.

When the 2012 baseball season began, current voice of the Razorbacks Chuck Barrett pointed out to writer Matt Jones of *Hawgs Illustrated*, "Five years ago you couldn't get an AM radio station to carry 30 games. Now you have 100,000-watt stations in Fort Smith and Little Rock carrying the majority of the games. Those are also sports-talk radio stations, so the baseball team has become part of the every-day conversation among Razorback fans in the spring."

Even though the total number of stations has declined, the potential audience for broadcasts is probably larger than ever. Several reasons account for the decline in the number of stations. Some of the stations, such as KFFA in Helena, have been part of the network since the beginning. But many stations are now owned by large chains and are locked into programming and advertising schedules that don't allow for special broadcasts. Some have gone to automated, pre-recorded weekend formats. And, of course, most Razorback football and basketball games, and an increasing number of events from other sports, are now available on television. Whereas radio was once the only source for live, on-the-spot coverage, there are a variety of alternatives now, including online coverage. But many Razorback fans, even for games carried on television, still tune in to the radio broadcasts. And even those attending the games, especially football and baseball, often bring their miniature radios with them so as to be able to listen to the voices of the Razorbacks while watching the game.

After the January 2012 Cotton Bowl in which Arkansas defeated Kansas State, many Arkansas fans who watched the national TV coverage on Fox complained that the TV announcers were either biased in favor of Kansas State or not well informed about the Razorbacks. And a number of them called radio talk shows to say they had turned off the TV volume and listened to the radio coverage on the Razorback network.

Along the same lines, some Arkansas fans, much preferring the Razorback radio broadcast to the ESPN television announcers at the 2012 baseball College World Series, devised a way to briefly delay the telecast on their video recorders so that it was synched up with the radio broadcast, which was a few seconds ahead of the telecast. That way they could have the video accompanied by the description and commentary from Chuck Barrett and Rick Schaeffer.

On a game day or night, it is still common to hear the broadcast of Razorback games clearly audible in stores and other places of business around the state. For a few years, Razorback football games were also available in Spanish-language broadcasts and that might return in the future.

Notable too is that thousands in Arkansas follow the Hogs through the media even though many of them are not UA alumni and have had no direct connection with the university. "I'm a t-shirt fan of the Hogs," said Rick Fahr, who grew up in eastern Arkansas and was editor of the *Log Cabin Democrat* in Conway. "I didn't attend the university. No one in my immediate family did. But ever since I could tune a radio or catch a few minutes of

KATV broadcasts, I've been a Razorbacks fan." Fahr went on, "I'm not alone. The Razorbacks belong to the entire state. There are fans in every city and town. We live and die by great wins—any over LSU will do—and heartbreaking losses." In a column after the overtime loss to the University of Louisiana at Monroe in the disappointing 2012 football season, Fahr wrote, "As the Razorbacks go, so goes a good portion of the state's giddyup. Win, it's quick and spry. Lose, it's ho-stinkin'-hum. It wasn't the University of Arkansas that lost a game Saturday night. It was a couple million Arkansans."

A similar perspective was offered by Ryan Hughes, publisher of *Vertical Arkansas* magazine. "Growing up in Arkansas, you are undoubtedly raised to call the Hogs. Every fall—from as far back as I can remember—I have supported the beloved Razorbacks. Going to games, cheering them on from my living room or listening to the game on the radio when Paul Eells would shout 'Oh my!'—while literally calling the Hogs on the front porch of my deer camp with a bunch of other grown men was part of my upbringing," Hughes recalled.

Many Razorback fans are also regular readers of *Hawgs Illustrated*, the magazine entirely devoted to Razorback news and features. Started in 1992 by publisher Clay Henry, it comes out 20 times year, including weekly during football seasons. There is also a *Hawgs Illustrated* website.

In 1951, Bob Cheyne, who had recently become the first sports publicity director at the University of Arkansas, crisscrossed the state to visit radio stations. Cheyne's goal was to establish a statewide radio network for Razorback sports. By the end of his tour, he had enlisted 34 stations to participate in the new venture. That statewide tour by Cheyne, who was accompanied by his wife, provided the foundation for what would become an enduring feature of life in Arkansas. Although an announcer today may say, "This is the Razorback Sports Network from IMG College," the Arkansas broadcast network still is a direct descendant of the Razorback network Cheyne assembled in the early 1950s.

1. Beginnings: 1940s and '50s

The first regular broadcasts of Razorback football games came in 1944. Bob Fulton, a Philadelphia native who had first come to Arkansas to attend the College (now University) of the Ozarks in Clarksville, began broadcasting football and basketball games for CBS on three radio stations in the state: KLRA in Little Rock, KXLR in North Little Rock, and KWEM in West Memphis. Fulton did play-by-play, and George Mooney of Knoxville, Tennessee, did color commentary for those early broadcasts. Both Fulton and Mooney later went on to long and successful sports broadcasting careers.

The University of Arkansas was a member of the Southwest Conference (SWC) for much of its sports history, having been part of the SWC from the league's foundation in 1914 until the Razorbacks moved to the Southeastern Conference (SEC) in 1992. Humble Oil and Refining Co. of Texas had long sponsored radio broadcasts of SWC football, with the first Humble-sponsored broadcasts dating back to 1933. All the announcers were based in Texas, and since Humble operated only in Texas, the overwhelming emphasis was on the Texas schools then in the SWC, Arkansas being the lone non-Texas school in the league.

For most of that period, there were six Texas schools in the SWC. Texas Tech joined in 1956 and Houston in 1971, bringing the total of Texas schools in the conference to eight. The SWC disbanded in 1996, four years after Arkansas left the league.

In 1946, Humble purchased the rights to football broadcasts of the schools then in the SWC. The legendary Kern Tips, known for his colorful characterizations such as "malfunction at the junction" (which was how he described a fumbled handoff between a quarterback and a running back), was the lead announcer for the Humble broadcasts for 30 years. Working with him were Alec Chesser and, later, Connie Alexander. Although Humble did not operate in Arkansas, the company agreed to allow five stations in Arkansas to carry broadcasts of SWC games. Humble was affiliated with Standard Oil, which marketed under the Esso brand in Arkansas at the time.

The 1951 printed program for home Razorback football games featured a full-page ad, "The Razorbacks Are On the Air!" The ad said, "If you can't drive to all the Arkansas games, join the Razorback Radio Rooters, at home! Listen to the thrilling play-by-play broadcasts. If you can drive to the games, stop in at the Esso sign." Stations KGRH in Fayetteville, KFSA in Fort Smith, and KBRS in Springdale had ads in the 1951 program proclaiming that they were carrying broadcasts of the football games.

Eventually, Esso and Humble were joined together under the Exxon brand. The Humble-Esso-Exxon radio network continued to cover SWC games until 1978 when the oil company ended its sponsorship. The Mutual Broadcasting System, a national radio network, then took over the SWC broadcasts for five years, before Host Communications, based in Lexington, Kentucky, bought the rights in 1983. That year there was a separate SWC Radio Network operated by Host, which included some Arkansas stations. Arkansas, however, relied primarily on its own broadcast network.

John Barnhill, Bob Cheyne, and the Plan

The real beginning of Razorback broadcasting was set in motion when John Barnhill became the football coach and athletic director at Arkansas in 1946. He recognized the importance of getting people all over Arkansas to identify with the Razorbacks. Barnhill rejuvenated the football program, luring such players as Clyde "Smackover" Scott, who later became an All-American and earned a silver medal in the 110-meter high hurdles in the 1948 Olympics, and Leon "Muscles" Campbell to Fayetteville. Barnhill coached that 1946 team to a Southwest Conference championship and a berth in the Cotton Bowl.

When the 1948 football season opened, interest in the Razorbacks had risen to an all-time high. The 1947 season had concluded with a victory over William and Mary in the Dixie Bowl played in Birmingham, Alabama. A major event in Razorback history was the opening in Little Rock in September 1948 of War Memorial Stadium, which was to become the second home for the Razorbacks. Up to that point, Arkansas had played some of its games at Little Rock High School's 10,000-seat Tiger Stadium, later named Quigley Stadium.

Razorback Stadium in Fayetteville, the team's primary home, was originally built as a Works Progress Administration (WPA) project and dedicated in 1938. (The WPA was a Franklin Delano Roosevelt–era New Deal agency that provided jobs and undertook major public works projects around the country during the Great Depression.) Razorback Stadium initially had a capacity of about 13,500. By 1947, that had been boosted to 16,000. That year Arkansas played its home game against the University of Texas in Memphis, Tennessee, whose Crump Stadium could hold up to 32,000 fans. Scheduling that game in Memphis was seen by some as a move to pressure support for building War Memorial Stadium in Little Rock.

War Memorial had an initial capacity of 31,000. A crowd of 24,950, a record attendance at the time for a sports event in the state, watched the first game there on September 18, 1948, as Arkansas defeated Abilene Christian College 40–6. In subsequent years the Little Rock stadium on Markham Street was to be the site of many memorable Razorback games.

Over the years, stadium capacity at the stadiums in Little Rock (54,000-plus) and Fayetteville (72,000-plus) increased significantly as did interest in the Razorbacks. Broadcast coverage also increased, which in turn did much to stimulate that interest. Although today both stadiums are at or near capacity for Razorback games, many thousands of other fans are listening to or watching broadcasts of the game.

By 1950, John Barnhill, who was having health problems (later diagnosed as multiple sclerosis), had retired from coaching the Razorbacks but remained as athletic director. In 1950, he called Bob Cheyne into his office to ask if he could put together an Arkansas sports radio network if Humble Oil and the Southwest Conference would agree to grant permission. Barnhill knew that many in Arkansas were unable to hear Razorbacks games regularly, and he was determined to put the Razorbacks into every home in the state to build fan support and boost recruiting.

Cheyne, who had been a Navy journalist during World War II, became the University of Arkansas's first official sports publicity director (later sports information director) in July 1948. His first Razorbacks game in that role had been the dedication of War Memorial Stadium that year.

Humble Oil gave the go-ahead to the Arkansas plan if the Arkansas network would stay out of Texas. It was then that Cheyne began the process of assembling the statewide radio network, taking the leading role in getting the broadcasts on the air. In subsequent years, the network was to build an extraordinary presence in the state, which would prove to be a powerful connection that would greatly heighten interest in and support for Razorback sports.

Some of the Razorbacks' greatest players—such as football stars Barry Switzer, Ken Hatfield, and Jim Lindsey—have noted that they developed interest in playing for Arkansas by listening to radio broadcasts as boys. Interestingly, those three all came from eastern and southern Arkansas where, until broadcasts became available, there had been limited interest in the Razorbacks.

Bob Cheyne Gets Things Started

One of Bob Cheyne's first steps in establishing the Razorback network was to call Russell McKinney, who was the general manager of the Southwestern Bell phone company in Arkansas. As it was through the use of telephone lines that the operation of the network was set up, McKinney was a key figure in helping make the network operational.

At the time, as Cheyne explained, "You purchased use of a telephone line. If you were going to broadcast a game from Little Rock and you were going to go to Russellville, you purchased the time on that telephone line. So the more stations you were able to get in the network, the cheaper you will get it done." Cheyne recollected that there were at least 34 AM radio stations in

Arkansas then. "So, figuring, after spending some time with Russell [McKinney] and him fully explaining to me the operation of a network by way of telephone lines, I got in the car with my wife, Jennie. She was from North Little Rock, so we kind of made Little Rock our base. And I visited all 34 stations in the state."

Nearly 50 years later, Cheyne recalled, "I went up first of all and visited KDRS in Paragould. I can almost recall all of those stations—Ted Rand of KDRS in Paragould, Harold Sudbury of KLCN in Blytheville. I visited a Little Rock station. I just circled the state. I visited northeast Arkansas and came back to Little Rock for the night. Then I did eastern Arkansas and met Sam Anderson at KFFA at Helena. Then I went over to Forrest City and met Bill Fogg at KXJK, then I went down to Crossett to visit Julian Haas, and over to El Dorado and then I went to southwest Arkansas and visited a Texarkana, Arkansas, station. And there was station KAMD in Camden." This venture took the better part of a week, Cheyne said. Although his visits to the stations were unannounced, many of the stations put him on the air to talk about the Razorbacks.

The prices Cheyne offered to the stations for carrying the broadcasts pale in comparison to the big business atmosphere that prevails in collegiate sports today and the connections that Arkansas sports have with major national networks and IMG.

At the end of that 1951 tour, Cheyne said that all 34 stations were interested in being on the network. "That would give us total coverage in Arkansas." He met again with McKinney and gave him a list of the stations. "I would have two stations in Little Rock...two in Fort Smith, two in El Dorado at the time, and two in the Fayetteville-Springdale area." Cheyne calculated that the stations could be included in the network for $25 a game, with the Little Rock stations paying $50. The stations would retain any profit from advertising. Cheyne said he also got permission from Athletic Director Barnhill to offer each station two complimentary tickets to every in-state football game. "I mean, you couldn't do that today," he commented. "And they were ecstatic about it." As Cheyne pointed out, those fees for being part of the network are unbelievably low by today's standards.

Part sports reporter, part Razorback booster, part entrepreneur, and part traveling salesman, Cheyne, with assistance from McKinney—and backed up by the enthusiastic response from Arkansas broadcasters and the support of Barnhill—had established the framework for a statewide Razorbacks network. "I'm sure that these stations at that time sold the games [to advertisers] for at least $100 or maybe $125 a game. So they were all making a profit, a good profit, and Arkansas finally was totally covered by Razorback football. And I think every coach I've worked with since then would tell you this—that nothing contributed to the interest, including ticket sales, in Razorback football more than having a statewide network. People could finally hear the Razorbacks."

Prior to that time, as Cheyne pointed out, Arkansas lost some great football players to colleges in other states. He mentioned specifically Paul "Bear" Bryant from Fordyce and Ken Kavanaugh of Little Rock, who starred for Alabama and LSU, respectively, in the 1930s. Another who left the state was John "Kayo" Dottley, a fullback from McGehee who starred at Ole Miss, breaking rushing records and becoming an All-American in 1949. "We would lose players, outstanding players, some of whom would become great All-Americans, because there wasn't that much interest in Razorback football," Cheyne said. " In eastern and southern Arkansas, they were closer to Alabama. They were closer to Mississippi. They couldn't receive Razorback football broadcasts, and the only ones covering them at that time were people like Orville Henry of the *Gazette*." Henry began regularly covering the Razorbacks in 1945.

"So, I say unequivocally that the establishment—I'm not taking credit for this thing—I'm talking about the radio...what we called the University of Arkansas Sports Network in 1951, did more to create interest in Razorback football than anything else," Cheyne said with obvious pride.

Cheyne had made a whirlwind tour of the state and the result was that Razorback games would now be heard throughout Arkansas, creating dreams in the minds of youngsters of playing for the Razorbacks and building a passionate following in all corners of the state.

Upon receiving an honorary degree from the University of Arkansas at the 2011 commencement ceremony, Alan Sugg, who served as president of the UA system from 1990 to 2011, recalled that, as a boy growing up in Helena (on the far side of the state from Fayetteville), he listened to Razorback football games with his dad, with Wallie Ingalls announcing. Sugg, who attended the university on a track scholarship as a pole vaulter, said that it was those football broadcasts that first attracted him to UA. His is one of many similar stories.

Frank W. Oldham Jr., who grew up in northeast Arkansas—and who served on the university's Board of Trustees, 1990–2000, and as chairman, 1998–2000—remembers listening to Razorback football games at an early age in his dad's pickup, which had an antenna that could receive the broadcast when the family radio could not.

Bob Cheyne's Impact

Bob Cheyne was a relative newcomer to Arkansas, but he made a significant impact. "I grew up in Chicago and moved to Little Rock in 1942 when my dad became USO director," Cheyne said. (The United Service Organizations—USO—played an important role during World War II in providing recreation services for uniformed military personnel.) Cheyne got out of the U.S. Navy in 1946 and the following year, at age 20, he became sports editor of the *Northwest Arkansas Times* in Fayetteville. The next year, he became the sports publicity director at the university. The 1949 Razorback media guide stated, "Bob Cheyne, sports publicity director at Arkansas, joined the athletic department staff in July 1948. Cheyne has had two years of newspaper experience in addition to 18 months with service newspapers in the Navy. In addition to Razorback publicity, he is sports editor of the *Razorback Review*, an alumni weekly published in the fall."

Cheyne gives credit to Barnhill for establishing a foundation for broadening interest in Razorback sports, particularly football. Winning a Southwest conference championship in his first season in 1946 helped set the stage for success. "He had great players like Clyde Scott, Leon "Muscles" Campbell, and Eugene "Bud" Canada, an end from Hot Springs and later a state senator for many years." That season concluded with Arkansas and LSU playing to a 0–0 draw in a legendary Cotton Bowl game on a frigid day in Dallas with the playing field covered in snow and ice.

As interest in Arkansas football began to increase, Cheyne said that people began deluging Barnhill with letters: *When are we going to be able to hear Razorback football? We have to drive 30 miles. Or, We have to drive this far to pick up a Little Rock station. Or, We can't get it at all, and when are we going to be able to get Razorback football broadcasts?*

"People were interested, and the only way many of them could follow it was either drive somewhere or read Orville Henry's column," Cheyne explained. "It was hurting our ticket sales. It was hurting our fan interest. For years it had a devastating effect upon our recruiting. When you hear kids today down at Warren or Forrest City asked why they became a Razorback, they say, 'I've always wanted to be a Razorback.' It's because they've been able to follow it." He contrasts this to the earlier period when too many potential Razorbacks wound up at universities in surrounding states.

Cheyne got his start at the UA in the spring of 1948. Deke Brackett, who was the backfield coach under Barnhill, had also been charged with reviving the university's baseball program, which had been discontinued from 1930 to 1946. Cheyne said Brackett asked him, "Would you cover our baseball schedule and come with the team if we pay your expenses?" Cheyne got approval of Ted Wiley, editor of the *Times*, to cover the baseball team. Brackett was pleased with Cheyne's work and recommended to Barnhill that he hire Cheyne as the sports publicity director, later called sports information director.

Cheyne noted that others at the university, particularly Walter J. Lemke, had previously helped publicize the university and its sports teams. Professor Lemke was the founder and longtime head (1928–1959) of the university's journalism department, which was named in his honor in 1988. In fact, Lemke played a role in helping the first Razorback football player to be named as an All-American. Wear Schoonover, a pre-law student from Pocahontas, was an outstanding player as an end on both offense and defense. (He also lettered in basketball, baseball, and track.) However, Schoonover was little known nationally until Lemke began a publicity campaign on his behalf. At the end of the 1929 season, Schoonover was named as an All-American at a time when only 11 players were chosen for that honor. He often credited Lemke for helping him to achieve that distinction.

Cheyne was the first UA sports publicist to work directly for the athletic department. When he took the job, Cheyne said, "I had a part-time secretary. I had a manually operated mimeograph machine. I sent out three or four releases every week, three to four pages long—all had to be typed upon stencils. On stencils, if you made an error, you got a paperclip, dabbed a little ink on it and rubbed over it." Cheyne notes that the stencils were a far cry from today's computerized communication. And in those early days, he hand-folded the releases and sent them out to the press. He added, "I had a mailing list of about 150 to 200 who got those releases" three or four times per week.

He remembers that the first press release he sent out was about Clyde Scott going to the Olympics. "In 1948, the Olympics were resumed after a break of 12 years because of World War II, and they were to be held in London. And Clyde had won the NCAA championship in the 110-yard high hurdles." Scott finished second in the event at London, taking the silver medal. Cheyne called him "one of the mildest men and greatest athletes that I've ever known."

Although Cheyne began as sports publicity or information director, he would eventually expand his duties to take on some of the broadcast responsibilities, becoming one of the early voices of the Razorbacks on the radio network he had helped establish. Cheyne first did some work with Bob Fulton, who had previously announced Razorback games for the few CBS stations in the state. Fulton would later gain national prominence as an announcer for Mutual Radio's baseball game of the day, and he served as the radio voice of the South Carolina Gamecocks for 43 years before retiring in 1995. He died in 2010 at age 89. Cheyne called Fulton "one of the greatest voices I ever heard in sports."

Cheyne's first on-air experience was for a basketball halftime report. "I was working with the basketball team, and all I was doing, as SID (Sports Information Director) was keeping statistics," Cheyne recalled. During a commercial break, Fulton asked if Cheyne would take over the broadcast during halftime and report statistics. Cheyne agreed and did that regularly until Fulton left in 1952. Fulton remembered that all Razorbacks football games in Fayetteville when he was broadcasting were played in the afternoon in a small stadium with no lights. He also remembered that the drive from Little Rock to Fayetteville was about 200 miles and could be challenging when there was snow. "I would have to get the state police to get me through."

Bob Fulton's Pioneer Broadcasting

Although Fulton grew up in Pennsylvania, he attended the College of the Ozarks (now the University of the Ozarks), a Presbyterian school in Clarksville, Arkansas. He had a small scholarship through the Presbyterian Church. After college, Fulton remained in Arkansas, coaching basketball and football at Hartman High and later at Pulaski Heights Junior High in Little Rock. Fulton then got a job at radio station KLRA in Little Rock and began his broadcasting career announcing Little Rock (later Central) High School football and basketball. There were no exclusive rights to Razorback football broadcasts at the time and he soon moved up to announcing Razorbacks games for the CBS stations in Arkansas.

Fulton recalled that in 1948, when he married his wife, Dody, "We spent the first night of our marriage in Heber Springs. Then, we did a basketball game in Fayetteville, and stayed in the Mountain Inn (where visiting basketball teams usually stayed). Two nights later, we went to Tulsa and I did a game there. In other words, our honeymoon was designed around basketball."

By that time, he had worked for a station in West Memphis and then moved to North Little Rock with KXLR, a Mutual network station. "The University of Arkansas had begun to award exclusive rights to its football broadcasts and KXLR was the anchor station," Fulton said.

While still living in Little Rock, Fulton began to spend summers announcing baseball, working in locations as diverse as Pueblo, Colorado, and Hornell, New York. Then he got the job in 1952 as radio announcer for the Columbia, South Carolina, Reds, a minor league club in the South Atlantic (Sally) League. With that came the opportunity to announce University of South Carolina football and basketball. The Columbia job also led to his being hired by Mutual in 1954 to broadcast major league baseball games.

Fulton remembered that the first Razorbacks football game he broadcast was the Texas game in 1944, played in Little Rock at the high school stadium, a 19–0 Texas victory, before a crowd of about 10,000, which was a big turnout during wartime. He was also behind the microphone at the first game played in War Memorial Stadium in 1948. "At one time, I was calling several games a week," he said. "I would do a junior high game on Thursday, a high school game on Friday night, an Arkansas game on Saturday afternoon, and an Arkansas Intercollegiate Conference game on Saturday night. As if that wasn't enough, on Sunday afternoon I would do a re-creation of Philadelphia Eagles games." Those Eagles games were of interest in Arkansas because Clyde Scott was playing for the NFL team.

Re-Creation Broadcasts

Radio re-creations are a lost art today, but were once a regular feature of sports broadcasting. The announcers would broadcast from a studio rather than from the site of the game being broadcast, often some distance away. Because of the costs involved for travel, phone connections, etc., many radio stations would "re-create" game coverage when the local team was playing away from home. The announcer in the studio would receive a brief, terse telegraph account of what was happening in a game. He would then provide a creative narrative of the game for his listening audience, many of whom did not know that the announcer was not actually present at the game. This was especially common in baseball coverage.

Broadcasters used crowd noise sound effects and simulated the sounds of bats hitting balls. Because of the process involved, these broadcasts often ran well behind the time of the actual game and sometimes, when there were breakdowns or delays in the telegraph transmissions, announcers described a rain delay when, in fact, weather at the game site was sunny and bright. Although re-creations were primarily used for baseball, the practice was also utilized for some football games, such as the Eagles games Fulton did. Among those who did re-creations was Ronald Reagan, who did some football as well as baseball broadcasts early in his career which, of course, would eventually lead to the White House.

One of the last of the broadcasters to do re-creations was Jim Elder, who was the voice of the Arkansas Travelers minor league baseball team from 1965 to 1993. Elder, like Fulton, was a Pennsylvania native. For some years, he described Travelers' road games from a Little Rock studio, aided by a library of sound effects. Earlier, he had been a minor league umpire and in 1951 was the general manager of the Hot Springs Bathers minor league baseball team in the old Class C Cotton States League.

Elder later served as the longtime statistician for Razorbacks football broadcasts, a position he held from 1970 until his death in 1998. Writer Harry King remembered how, during Razorback games, Elder greatly aided the announcers by coming up with his own index card system, with easy access to a player's past performance, such as yards on a return or the length of previous field goals made or missed. His statistical mastery was an important behind-the-scenes part of Razorback broadcasts. Elder's encyclopedic knowledge of the Razorbacks made him a popular host for Little Rock radio sports shows for many years.

Fulton said that doing the re-creations of the Philadelphia Eagles football games for Arkansas stations "proved to be a valuable education, because it gave me experience in doing re-creations based on feeds from Western Union operators, who would telegraph only the basic information." In his autobiography, co-authored with Don Barton (Hi, Everybody! This is Bob Fulton), Fulton said he would add in "extracurricular action" and color commentary.

Bob Fulton: National Broadcasts and South Carolina

Bob Fulton's diverse experience in Arkansas and elsewhere helped prepare him for his national broadcasting role with the Mutual Game of the Day when he worked with some of the best-known sports announcers and baseball personalities of the era. Mutual had a network of 450 radio stations nationwide and could reach audiences of 35 million or more. Among those involved with Fulton in the Mutual broadcasts was Dizzy Dean, the Arkansas farm boy who had been a star pitcher for the St. Louis Cardinals.

However, Fulton decided after a year (1954) of doing the Game of the Day that, with a young family at home, he didn't want to do the constant traveling for national baseball coverage and settled into his job of broadcasting South Carolina football and basketball. He was not entirely finished with the Razorbacks, however. In late 1961, Cheyne called his old friend to ask if he would fill in for him. The Arkansas team was playing in the Poinsettia Basketball Classic in Greenville, South Carolina, but the two games there were taking place just before UA's football team was to play Alabama in the Sugar Bowl, and Cheyne had to be in New Orleans for that. So Fulton agreed to do the play-by-play of Arkansas basketball games against Clemson and Georgia Tech for the Arkansas radio network.

After Arkansas and South Carolina joined the Southeastern Conference and began playing each other in football in 1992, Fulton was the play-by-play announcer for the games between the Gamecocks and Razorbacks for several years. The first contest, in 1992, was a 45–7 Arkansas victory, a bittersweet experience for Fulton.

Fulton became one of the legendary announcers in college athletics. His career broadcasting for South Carolina football, basketball, and baseball spanned from 1952 to 1964 and 1967 to 1995. "I don't know that I am 'a legend,'" Fulton said shortly before his death. "What I always tried to do was to give the listeners as fair a representation of the games as I could."

Wallie Ingalls Behind the Mike

With Fulton in South Carolina, the broadcasting duties for the new Arkansas network had been taken over by Cheyne and Wallie Ingalls, with Ingalls becoming the first regular play-by-play announcer for Razorbacks football on the newly established UA network, beginning with the 1952 season.

By 1956, the Arkansas media guide published by Cheyne said that no other school in the country could claim as extensive an in-state network of radio stations for its entire ten-game football schedule. "Founded some four-and-half years ago as an answer to inadequate radio coverage for Razorback games, the University of Arkansas Sports Network last year had an affiliate in every city in the entire state where a radio station was located," the guide said. "In addition, key stations immediately outside the state's boundaries were included to give the network a potential listening audience of over three million people." The guide noted that Cheyne directed the network's operations and pointed out that, during the past school year, "the network also broadcast the spring Red-White game to a network of some 20 stations and in addition became the first to air over a two-state network the complete results of a Southwest Conference track and field meet."

In 1956, at age 39, Ingalls was entering his fifth season as the football play-by-play announcer for the Razorbacks. Ingalls was also program and sports director of station KGRH in Fayetteville and broadcast Fayetteville High School games. He was a graduate of Carnegie Tech in Pittsburgh and the starting fullback for the 1939 Sugar Bowl team. (Carnegie Tech later became part of Carnegie Mellon University and discontinued participation in major intercollegiate sports). Ingalls had also worked as a high school coach before beginning his stint as announcer for the Razorback broadcasts.

Grant Hall, longtime Northwest Arkansas sports journalist, said his first memories of Razorback broadcasting include hearing Ingalls doing play-by-play in the mid-1950s. "He had a lot of great, old-style sayings, like referring to a young player as a 'speed merchant' if the player could run really fast. Or he would say that a halfback would only weigh 162 pounds 'soaking wet.'" Ingalls was also known for his trademark sign-off of broadcasts: "Win, lose, or draw, let's be sports about it."

The 1956 media guide touted the scheduled television coverage of the Arkansas–Texas Christian game in Fort Worth on October 13, which it said was the third appearance on national TV for the Razorbacks, but the first complete UA regular season game to be covered. (Arkansas lost that game 41–6.) In fact, a very small audience had been able to watch the televised 1948 Arkansas game at TCU in Fort Worth. WBAP-TV in Fort Worth received permission from the Southwest Conference to televise the game, which Arkansas, led by Clyde Scott, won 27–14. Television was in its infancy at that time and there were only about 2,000 TV sets in the Dallas–Fort Worth area.

The first national appearance for the Razorbacks was in 1953, when about one-third of the 1953 Arkansas–Ole Miss game in Memphis was shown on a national panorama, switching back and forth between four different games. And the Cotton Bowl match-up with Georgia Tech on January 1, 1955, was nationally televised.

The Wondrous 1954 Season

That Cotton Bowl game came at the end of the wondrous 1954 season that did so much to build excitement around Razorback football. Coach Bowden Wyatt's "25 Little Pigs" reeled off seven consecutive wins, several of them dramatic upsets, and were ranked as high as fourth nationally during the season.

As the *Arkansas Gazette*'s Orville Henry wrote at the time, the 1954 team, which finished the season as number ten in the Associated Press national poll, "gained more national acclaim than any previous Porker squad including the Passing-est teams of 1936-37." The Razorbacks were featured several times in *Sports Illustrated*, the then-new national sports magazine. The November 1, 1954, issue of *Sports Illustrated* had a major story, "Underdog Arkansas Wins Again," with pictures of the game-winning play out of the single-wing formation in the Razorbacks 6–0 win over Ole Miss. That play became known as the "Powder River Play" in Arkansas football lore, a name that came from Wyoming where Wyatt and some others on his staff had previously coached. The Powder River in Wyoming was said to be a mile wide and six inches deep. The Arkansas coaching staff decided that if the play was ever going to be used, this was the time for it.

Wyatt knew that if George Walker, the team's best passer, was in the game, Ole Miss would be expecting a pass on third and six. Instead, Buddy Bob Benson was in at the tailback position and he was a strong runner, so Ole Miss expected a run. Benson took the center snap and rolled out as if to run. Downfield, Preston Carpenter, who had come out of the backfield, faked a block on the defensive end and then eased by the Rebels' safety. As Benson neared the sideline, he lofted the pass to the wide-open Carpenter who took it in for the winning touchdown.

It was that legendary victory over Ole Miss that catapulted Arkansas into the national spotlight and—more than any other single game to that point—captured the state's affection. At the time, Arkansas and Ole Miss were not in the same conference, Ole Miss being in the Southeastern Conference, but they were longtime rivals. Going into the 1954 game, Ole Miss was considered a national power and a definite favorite. In an unusual twist, the game counted as an SEC conference game for Ole Miss because it had been unable to schedule the six SEC games required for eligibility for the conference championship.

Under the front-page banner headline, "Soo-ie! Razorbacks Do It Again," here's the way Orville Henry described the game in the *Gazette* of October 24, 1954:

> The keyed-up, unbeaten football teams of Arkansas and Mississippi rocked each other from end to end of War Memorial Stadium without issue for almost four periods yesterday afternoon.
>
> Then, with 3¾ minutes left on the clock, a gorgeous "home run" pass play won for the Razorbacks 6-0.
>
> Tailback Buddy Bob Benson threw a perfect strike for about 35 yards and Blocking Back Preston Carpenter took the ball over his shoulder without breaking stride and galloped another 35 yards.
>
> It went into the book as a 66-yard play from the line of scrimmage.

That same day, the entire front page of the *Gazette* sports section was devoted to a giant panoramic view of the packed War Memorial Stadium, with the headline, "38,000 Jam Stadium for Thriller." During that 1954 season, after a 20–7 win over the University of Texas at Austin, accounts of Razorback games began appearing on the front page of the Sunday *Arkansas Gazette* instead of in the sports section, and they remained a front-page fixture until the newspaper was bought out by the *Arkansas Democrat* in 1991—on the weekend of the last Arkansas-Texas Southwest Conference game.

The upturn in coverage in the *Gazette* started in 1946, when the Razorbacks won the SWC and went to the Cotton Bowl, said longtime sports writer Jim Bailey, "but the real breakthrough came in 1954" when Arkansas earned another trip to the Cotton Bowl and game stories started regularly appearing on page one.

Jim Lindsey, from Forrest City in eastern Arkansas, who later became a star for the Razorbacks, said he first became acquainted with Razorback football listening to the broadcast of that 1954 Ole Miss game. "I didn't go to the game but listened on the radio like thousands and thousands of other Arkansas fans. Arkansas won 6–0. Every Saturday thereafter we were glued to the radio, listening to our beloved Razorbacks."

As sports columnist Walter Stewart wrote in the *Memphis Commercial Appeal* after that Ole Miss game, "The Porkers were supposed to finish next to last in the Southwest Conference and here they are as undefeated as the United States Army."

When Buddy Bob Benson died in 2011, an account of his career in the *Arkansas Democrat-Gazette* referred to the game-winning pass against Ole Miss as "what many consider to be the most famous pass in Razorbacks history." Following his playing days at Arkansas, Benson, who was from De Queen, spent most of his career as a successful football coach at Ouachita Baptist University. And only a few months after Benson's death, Carpenter, who had a lengthy career in the NFL after being a first-round draft choice of the Cleveland Browns, also died around the same time, and news reports again emphasized the famous 1954 pass play and its importance in Arkansas football history. The headline in the *Arkansas Democrat-Gazette* when Carpenter died said, "Carpenter, who made '54 catch, dies at 77."

The 1954–55 edition of the *Razorback*, the UA student yearbook, described the Ole Miss game this way: "Before over 36,000 victory-starved fans the hell-for-leather Pigs from the hill fought on even terms with a powerhouse Ole Miss football machine for 56 minutes then went for broke and connected for their second shutout of the season." The yearbook paid tribute to the Arkansas defense: "Led by guards Bud Brooks and Eddie Bradford, they fought off each Rebel charge and boosted the Pigs into the fourth spot in the nation."

Years later, Bradford said Benson's pass to Preston Carpenter "put Arkansas into the contemporary era." And at later gatherings of teammates from 1954, Carpenter would joke that Benson's pass was a "dying quail." However, Benson, recalling the play for columnist Nate Allen, said, "I sprinted left and looked up and saw Preston down there and I threw it as far as I could. It was a 66-yard-pass. They say I threw it about three yards—actually it was about 30-something—and he went the rest of the way. He was back there all by himself."

The 1954 winning streak came to an end three weeks after the Ole Miss game in a 21–14 loss to SMU in Fayetteville. As *Sports Illustrated* reported, "Defeat at last came to a wonder team of Arkansas Razorbacks." That was followed by a 7–6 defeat at the hands of LSU of the Southeastern Conference. Nonetheless, the Razorbacks were Southwest Conference champions and Cotton Bowl bound.

Sports Illustrated had referred to the Razorbacks as the "Cinderella team of 1954," and an Associated Press poll of the nation's football experts ranked the Arkansas team as "the biggest surprise" of the 1954 season.

The media attention in 1954 also included national radio coverage in addition to the growing Arkansas radio network. The national coverage involved some of the greatest names in sports-broadcasting history. CBS, with Vin Scully doing the radio play-by-play, carried the Ole Miss game, and NBC, with Mel Allen and Curt Gowdy, broadcast the SMU contest. Scully, Allen, and Gowdy would become top TV sportscasters in later years. Scully became famed as the longtime radio and television voice of the Brooklyn and Los Angeles Dodgers. Allen was the play-by-play announcer for the New York Yankees for many years and broadcast Rose Bowl games as well as other top-flight sports events. Gowdy, who as a University of Wyoming basketball player saw action against Arkansas in the 1941 NCAA tournament, was well known as the longtime voice of the Boston Red Sox and for his coverage of many nationally televised sporting events, primarily for NBC Sports in the 1960s and '70s.

Before the November Homecoming game with SMU in Fayetteville, the *Arkansas Gazette* reported that coverage for the game would include three radio networks (including Mel Allen and NBC "coast to coast"); three TV stations; seven national newsreels; and around 31 newspapers from all over the South and Southwest. In addition, *Life* and *Sports Illustrated*, with Herman Hickman, would cover the game, the *Gazette* said. Hickman had been an All-American at Tennessee, later the coach at Yale, and one of the first TV football commentators.

At the end of that memorable season, another Hall of Fame sports broadcaster, Lindsey Nelson, and legendary football great Red Grange ("The Galloping Ghost") did the television coverage of the Cotton Bowl on January 1, 1955, for NBC. That was one of 26 Cotton Bowls Nelson covered. He also spent 17 years broadcasting the New York Mets and three years with the San Francisco Giants.

Wallie Ingalls was the man behind the microphone on the Razorback network for the 1954 season, providing the radio play-by-play during most of the 1950s, continuing in that role until 1959. Ingalls's role ended when he left the Fayetteville radio station where he had worked and accepted a marketing job, which was seen as a conflict with his Razorback responsibilities.

Charlie Jones Tries—and Succeeds—Elsewhere

One of those who sought to replace Ingalls as the Razorbacks broadcaster was Charlie Jones, a young man from Fort Smith. Jones had worked for KFPW, a Fort Smith station, and, along with a colleague, Jack Freeze, had broadcast many area sports events.

"I tried every year for five years to become the voice of the Razorbacks," Jones said. "Every spring, I would go see John Barnhill. I would have tapes, pictures, and a resume. I would sit down and tell him everything I had done that year." Following repeated failures to convince Barnhill to hire him, Jones said, after visiting Barnhill's office every year from 1955 through 1960, "I'm a slow learner, but it finally dawned on me that I wasn't going to get that job. That's really the job I wanted more than anything."

Although Jones, who received a law degree from Arkansas in 1953, failed to become the voice of the Razorbacks, he had a highly successful career in the top ranks of sports broadcasting. He had more luck with Lamar Hunt than with Barnhill. Hunt was one of the founders of the American Football League, which would become a rival of and then merge with the National Football League. Jones got in on the ground floor with Hunt and in 1960 became the original voice of the Dallas Texans, who would soon become the Kansas City Chiefs. Jones remembered that he arrived in Dallas for an interview with Hunt with only six dollars in his pocket, having driven from Texarkana where he covered a high-school basketball game. He had an 11 a.m. appointment with Hunt and, at the suggestion of his brother, Jones sent Hunt a clock set at 11 a.m. with this message: "The new voice of the Dallas Texans will be at your office at 11 a.m. Saturday." It apparently helped Jones get the job.

Altogether, Jones covered pro football for 37 years, working for both NBC and ABC. And his work went well beyond football. He got some early experience doing minor league baseball broadcasts with Bill Mercer for the Dallas-Fort Worth Spurs team in the Texas League and did studio re-creations when the team was on the road. Jones and Mercer had worked together on the Texans radio broadcasts until the team moved to Kansas City.

"I did ABC's first televised pro football game, which was the Dallas Texans versus the Los Angeles Chargers," Jones said. "The producer of that game was a curly-haired guy I had a lot of fun with—Roone Arledge. After the game, he complimented me on the job I did. I thanked him and told him it was the first TV game I had ever done. He said it was the first game he had ever produced."

As Jones pointed out, Arledge "turned out to be one of the great innovators of early sports TV." And Arledge was to figure importantly in one of the most memorable and significant Razorback football games, the 1969 "Great Shootout."

Jones worked with Arledge on ABC's pioneering TV sports show "Wide World of Sports" and was also involved in coverage of Wimbledon tennis, World Cup soccer, and the Olympics. He was the first announcer for the Colorado Rockies major league baseball franchise when it was established in 1993. Earlier he had done television coverage of baseball's Cincinnati Reds. In 1997, he was awarded the Pro Football Hall of Fame's Pete Rozelle Radio-Television Award. And in 1989 he was honored as a Distinguished Alumnus by the University of Arkansas Alumni Association.

Jones and Freeze, who later became mayor of Fort Smith, did get to fill in on a few Razorback games when Jones was still in Fort Smith. However, as Freeze said, "Charlie's ambition was to be the voice of the Razorbacks, but Barnhill wouldn't hire him. So, he went on to do ABC and NBC. He went straight to the top."

Jones did get to do television play-by-play for one big Arkansas football game—ABC's coverage of the 1969 UA Sugar Bowl victory over Georgia. Before that game, Jones was back in his home town of Fort Smith and prepped for the broadcast by meeting with some of the Razorback players.

Jones, who died in June 2008 at the age of 77, said earlier that year, "I've gotten to travel and see the world. I flew five million miles in 40 years…and covered 28 sports in 25 foreign countries."

"I've been really lucky," Jones added. "I would have been just as lucky and had just as much fun had I got that job at the University of Arkansas. You always look back at what might have been. I always figured you tried three times at something you wanted, then if it doesn't work out, move on and look for other opportunities." That's what Jones did, although he actually tried five times instead of three to get the Arkansas job.

Cheyne Takes the Broadcasting Role, and the Broyles Era Begins

One reason that Jones didn't get the Arkansas job is because Athletic Director Barnhill wanted to keep it "in house." And who better to do the Razorback broadcasts than Bob Cheyne, who had started the Arkansas network? Although Cheyne had recommended that Jones be considered, he said Barnhill told him, "Bob, I'd like to just keep it here, rather than go outside for someone. You know the coaches. You know the people. It would just make it easier on everybody." Years later, Cheyne said that when he had recommended Jones to Barnhill, the athletic director asked him where Jones was from. When Cheyne said that Jones was from Fort Smith, Barnhill replied, "We're not hiring any outsiders."

Cheyne took over the play-by-play announcing in addition to his other responsibilities. He began announcing basketball in the 1958–59 season and football in the fall of 1959.

In the meantime, Arkansas experienced football coaching changes. Following the breakthrough 1954 season, Arkansas fans presented Wyatt with a new Cadillac and a check for $15,300.

However, Wyatt, who was notoriously unavailable to the press, soon decamped for his alma mater, Tennessee. As the story goes, he got in the Cadillac that appreciative Razorback supporters had bought for him after that memorable season and drove it to Knoxville, where he became head coach at the school where he had been an All-American end in 1938.

Wyatt was replaced at Arkansas by Jack Mitchell, who had been a star split-T quarterback at Oklahoma and was coaching at Wichita, his first head coaching job. Mitchell had three winning, though not spectacular, seasons at Arkansas, with his teams going 5–4–1, 6–4, and 6–4. There were some key wins such as victories over Texas in 1955 and 1956 and Ole Miss in 1956 and 1957, and enthusiasm for Razorback football continued to build. However, at the end of the 1957 season, Mitchell was lured back to his native state of Kansas to take the coaching job at KU.

Athletic Director John Barnhill (left), pictured with Otis Douglas, Razorback football coach 1950–1952. Barnhill played a major role in getting Razorback games broadcast around the state.

Bob Cheyne played the leading role in establishing the Razorback network and was also a longtime voice of Razorback broadcasting.

Bob Cheyne in the press box broadcasting booth, where he spent many hours broadcasting and directing coverage of Razorback games on the network he helped set in motion.

As much as any play or any game, the 66-yard touchdown pass to Preston Carpenter from Buddy Bob Benson to defeat Ole Miss 6–0 in 1954 bolstered interest in Razorback football. Radio listeners throughout the state thrilled to the victory and more and more fans began tuning in to Razorback games.

An ad in the 1951 football program tells those who couldn't attend every game that they could hear games on Fort Smith and Springdale radio stations and read about them in the Southwest-Times Record *newspaper.*

The RAZORBACKS
are On The Air!

If you can't drive to all the Arkansas games, join the Razorback Radio Rooters, *at home!* Listen to the thrilling play-by-play broadcasts.

If you *can* drive to the games, stop in at the ESSO sign. That's where you find the good things you need for your car, and *Happy Motoring.*

For up-to-the-minute headline news, tune in Your ESSO Reporter over KLRA-1010 Kc., every weekday at 8 A. M., 12 noon, and 5:45 P. M.

FREE!

Get your pocket-size Razorback schedule listing all Arkansas games, and the radio stations carrying the play-by-play broadcasts. It's FREE at your nearby ESSO dealer station. Ask for it!

ESSO STANDARD OIL COMPANY

This 1951 ad summoned "Razorback Radio Rooters" to listen to broadcasts sponsored by Esso gasoline (and Humble Oil) and offered a free pocket schedule listing the stations carrying the broadcasts.

A Million Listeners – U of A Sports Network

INGALLS

Probably no school in the United States can claim as extensive as in-state network of radio stations for its entire 10-game football schedule as does the University of Arkansas. Founded some four and a half years ago as an answer to inadequate radio coverage for Razorback games, the University of Arkansas Sports Network last year had an affiliate in every city in the entire state where a radio station was located. In addition, key stations immediately outside the state's boundaries were included to give the network a potential listening audience of over three million people.

The UofA Sports Network is an operation of the athletic department of the University—designed to insure low-cost grid and basketball coverage throughout the state on a non-exclusive basis. Directing its operation for the department is Bob Cheyne, sports publicity director. This past school year the network also broadcast the spring Red-White game to a network of some 20 stations and in addition—became the first to air over a two-state network the complete results of a Southwest Conference track and field meet.

Once again, for the fifth consecutive football season, the play-by-play will be handled by popular 39-year old Wallie Ingalls, program and sports director of Station KGRH, Fayetteville. Now practically a member of the department, Wallie is a graduate of Carnegie Tech and was the starting fullback for the 1939 Sugar Bowl team that faced Texas Christian that year. He has had a colorful post-college background that includes four seasons as a high school football and basketball coach in Ohio and 14 years of sports announcing.

A highlight of the 1956 season outside of the network will be the nation-wide television production of the Arkansas—Texas Christian game from Fort Worth on October 13. It will be the third appearance on national TV for the Razorbacks but the first complete regular season game to be seen. About one-third of the 1953 Arkansas—Ole Miss game was televised in a panorama and the Cotton Bowl classic with Georgia Tech was nationally televised on January 1, 1955. The Porkers have also been on radio nationally twice—on NBC (with Mel Allen and Curt Gowdy) against SMU in 1954, and on CBS (with Vin Scully) against Ole Miss that same year.

The Texas A&M game from College Station will be on regional television as part of the tremendous Humble Oil sports production in this conference. The Humble Oil Co., owns all SWC radio and TV rights in the state of Texas and provides several more million listeners to the Razorbacks in their league schedule.

Wallie Ingalls was the first regular play-by-play announcer for the Razorback network, which by 1956 could claim "a million listeners."

2. 1960s and Frank Broyles Era

Jack Mitchell's departure opened the way for a new and enduring chapter in Arkansas sports. Arkansas hired Frank Broyles, the highly regarded young coach at Missouri, who had been there only one year. Bob Cheyne remembers that John Barnhill "called me into his office in January 1958 and said, 'I don't want you to tell anybody about this, not even Jennie. I want you to go to Joplin in the morning and pick up Frank Broyles. He's flying in from Columbia (Missouri).'" At the time, Cheyne had been receiving numerous calls, particularly from Minnesota sports journalists, asking if Coach Murray Warmath at Minnesota was going to be the new coach. Warmath had been strongly rumored as a candidate, particularly because he, like Barnhill, had a Tennessee background. However, Barnhill had determined that Broyles was the man for the job.

Broyles, who had been a multi-sport star at Georgia Tech, playing quarterback for the legendary Coach Bobby Dodd, proved to be a perfect fit at Arkansas. There were some who were convinced that when Dodd retired at Georgia Tech, Broyles would return to coach at his alma mater. Cheyne recalled that one day Broyles called him into this office and said, "I want you to write out a statement and show it to me." He directed Cheyne to "make it very emphatic that I'm very complimentary about Coach Dodd" and what Dodd had meant to Broyles. But, Broyles said he wanted to make it clear: "I'm committed to stay in Arkansas for the rest of my career." Broyles then told Cheyne, "I want you to give me a copy. You just stick a copy in your wallet. And, when that news hits the paper that Coach Dodd is retiring, wherever you are, release it. If you're in Austin when it comes out, don't even call me, just release it." Cheyne said he kept that statement with him until the day Dodd's retirement was announced. Dodd retired from coaching after the 1966 season.

Broyles did, indeed, remain at Arkansas. He would spend 19 years coaching the Razorbacks, and he served as athletic director from 1973 through 2007. His teams had a 144–58–5 record from 1958 through 1976, making him the winningest and longest-tenured coach in UA history, and his teams played in ten bowl games. His undefeated 1964 team was ranked as the national champion by the Football Writers Association of America. As athletic director, he led Arkansas's move into the Southeastern Conference in 1990 (although Arkansas did not play an SEC football schedule until 1992).

Broyles became a television personality himself. He began appearing each Sunday afternoon during football season on *The Frank Broyles Show*, initially carried by KARK-TV in Little Rock and later by KATV in Little Rock and other stations around the state. Later, after retiring as coach, Broyles served as the TV analyst for ABC on college football telecasts from 1977 to 1985, working alongside longtime sportscaster Keith Jackson, not to be confused with Little Rock native Keith Jackson, a football star at Oklahoma and in the NFL, who later became the color analyst for Razorback football broadcasts.

Broyles, who won many honors as a player and coach, was also inducted into the Arkansas Sportswriters and Sportscasters Hall of Fame in 2011, in recognition of his outstanding work on the ABC college football telecasts. Broyles said he learned a lot from ABC's Keith Jackson. "He was a great teacher and friend to me."

He recalled that Jackson once asked him "after I tried to explain something and I became complicated and way too long, 'Frank, would your mother understand that?'" Broyles told Jackson that his mother probably would not have. Jackson told him, "Then, don't ever do it again!"

"I think I had great preparation for TV work because of my working relationships with both Orville Henry and Bud Campbell," Broyles said when he was inducted into the Arkansas Sportswriters and Sportscasters Hall of Fame. "They both played a role in getting me ready because I learned to explain the game for those that hadn't played. In what Orville wrote, it was so readable for our whole state....Bud helped me understand how to do that on my TV show. You have to learn not to talk in coaching terms." Broyles joined Eells, Campbell, Jim Elder, and Pat Summerall as sportscasters enshrined in the hall established by Conway's Arkansas Sports Club. Writers honored included Henry, Jim Bailey, Harry King, and Jerry McConnell, all of whom covered the Razorbacks.

While Broyles was coaching the Razorbacks, his Sunday show, in which he showed game highlights and discussed the previous and upcoming games, became a must-watch for Arkansas fans. The host for those programs in the early years was Claude (Bud) Campbell, who had gone to work as sports director for Little Rock's KARK-TV in 1954, then moved to KATV in 1966. He had also done Arkansas Travelers baseball games on radio from 1960 to 1966. (He was at the ballpark in Little Rock for the home games, but the road games were re-creations.) And Campbell had hosted a popular Southwest Conference football highlights TV show with SWC football official Cliff Shaw.

Campbell became a familiar figure to Razorbacks followers and in 1966 succeeded Bob Cheyne as the radio play-by-play announcer. Cheyne continued on the broadcast team as a color analyst along with George Walker, former Razorback quarterback. Entering that 1966 season, Cheyne had been involved in media coverage of 187 UA football games, 425 basketball games, and had edited more than 75 publications on the Razorbacks. He had been selected as Arkansas's Sportscaster of the Year for the previous four seasons.

Memorable Games and Broadcasts of the 1960s

Bob Cheyne had many memorable experiences in broadcasting Razorback games and in directing sports information operations at the university. The national championship football season of 1964 was certainly a highlight. In that championship season, the Arkansas Radio Network had grown to 80 stations, which included several from surrounding states.

As was often the case during that era, the Arkansas-Texas game in 1964 was a decisive one. When the two teams met in Austin on October 17, Texas was the defending national champion and ranked number one nationally, and Arkansas was ranked eighth. Interest in the game was intense, but, hard as it is to imagine today, there was no live TV coverage. So, those Razorback fans unable to make the trip to Austin listened to the thrilling game on the radio. The members of the Arkansas congressional delegation, their staffs, and other Arkansas fans in the Washington DC area made arrangements through Cheyne to have a special telephone line hooked up so that they could hear the broadcast.

Arkansas won a stunning 14–13 victory over the top-ranked Longhorns on that October night, highlighted by Ken Hatfield's 81-yard punt return, one of the most celebrated runs in the Razorbacks' history. After the Texas win, the Razorbacks shut out their remaining five opponents in 1964 and then defeated Nebraska 10–7 in the Cotton Bowl. That Cotton Bowl game was the only time they appeared on national television in that national championship season.

Among the many listening to the radio broadcast of the 1964 Arkansas-Texas game were those attending a game between two smaller college teams in the old Arkansas Intercollegiate Conference (AIC). As happened on a number of occasions when the Razorbacks were playing at the same time as other Arkansas schools, many of those at a game in Russellville or Arkadelphia or elsewhere in the state were following the UA game on their small radios. When the Razorback broadcast described Hatfield making his fabled punt return in Austin, fans in the stands at Arkansas Tech stood up and cheered.

The following year, the Arkansas-Texas game was televised nationally. It was also a thriller. As Bob Wisener of the Hot Springs *Sentinel-Record* recalled, "NBC Sports carried the 1965 classic and Lindsey Nelson, the lead announcer, called it the best college game he ever witnessed." As Wisener remembered, "Arkansas burst ahead 20–0, then watched Texas go up 24–20 in the fourth quarter before pulling it out on an 80-yard drive that Jon Brittenum and Bobby Crockett etched their names into Razorback immortality." With that 27–24 win, Arkansas vaulted over Texas into the number-one national ranking and later settled in to the number-two national spot until losing to LSU in the

Cotton Bowl on January 1, 1966, a game that ended the 22-game winning streak for the Hogs and was televised on CBS.

Interest Keeps Building

"When I was broadcasting…I was doing color all of those years, but in 1959 began doing play-by-play in football and basketball," Bob Cheyne recalled. "I would get a stack of telegrams during my broadcast from people who were hearing the game while on deer hunting or pheasant hunting trips in South Dakota. And I have a friend living here in Bentonville today, who lived in New Mexico, and he had to drive 50 miles up to some place in New Mexico to pick up that 50,000-watt station (KAAY) in Little Rock."

"Our coverage became unbelievable by the sixties," Cheyne went on, "when we got the great rivalry with Texas, then we went to seven bowl games and won seven Southwest Conference championships, or shared them, during those years I broadcast."

In his day, Cheyne was the radio network director, producer, and play-by-play announcer. He also did a scoreboard show immediately after an afternoon game and before night games, with scores received from other games by Western Union telegraph service. He noted the contrast to today's game broadcasts and pre-game and post-game shows, in which responsibilities are divided between ten to 12 people.

By 1961, "the U of A's air-arm," as the media guide called the radio network, had 68 affiliate stations in seven states. "The U of A Sports Network is an operation of the athletic department available to all stations outside the state of Texas (where Humble holds exclusive coverage) on a local sponsorship basis," the guide stated, adding that it was the largest network of its kind in the United States.

One of the most significant changes in the growth of Razorback football during the post-war period "has been the tremendous increase in press, radio, and TV coverage," the 1961 guide pointed out, adding that "local interest in Razorback football has grown to national interest and national coverage in the past decade."

"If interest in Razorback football has been reflected in consistent growth at the turnstiles, its popularity has also been amazing in terms of radio coverage," the 1962 media guide proclaimed. After ten years of operation, the University of Arkansas Sports Network was "the largest university-controlled production of its kind in the nation." Razorback games in 1961 were regularly broadcast over a 72-station network that covered the south and southwest, and the guide said, "In addition, the Humble Oil Network of Texas (which owns all SWC radio rights) programmed Arkansas football over networks of 25–35 stations." The guide concluded that on a given Saturday, the potential listening audience may well go over the 20 million mark.

The football network of 72 stations in 1962 included 60 in Arkansas and a dozen in surrounding states. "The network is a year-round operation—offering stations in Arkansas the complete 24-game Razorback basketball program as well as broadcast of Red-White football games in the spring." Further, the football network included a weekly "Razorback Round-up" program with Coach Broyles. The basketball network of 16–20 stations was said to be one of the largest in the country for a complete collegiate season. Cheyne was still handling play-by-play for both football and basketball.

By 1967, Campbell was in his second year as play-by-play announcer for football with George Walker and Cheyne alongside him handling analysis and color.

In its 17th season, in 1968, the UA Sports Network once more claimed to be the largest of its kind in the nation, with nearly100 stations carrying the football broadcasts, literally blanketing Arkansas, and with stations in Missouri, Oklahoma, Tennessee, Louisiana, and Kansas also part of the network. The basketball network included 25 stations. Radio network programming had been expanded to include a weekly *Razorback Roundup* program, a *Razorback Report* show three times a week, and the scoreboard show on Saturdays.

As the sports publicity/information director, Cheyne also was in charge of press box operations at Fayetteville and Little Rock. The press box at Razorback Stadium in Fayetteville, which had been refurbished and expanded in 1950, was, according to the 1956 football media guide, awarded the Football Writers of America certificate of merit in 1956 and "is one of the southwest's finest in terms of working facilities and services." The three-story structure had a capacity of around 200 writers, broadcasters, cameramen, and allied persons.

Close Calls and Miscues

While serving as broadcaster and sports information director for the Razorbacks, Cheyne endured some harrowing experiences and scheduling snafus in trying to get games on the air—some of which he could laugh about in later years but that caused him headaches at the time. On one occasion he was scheduled to broadcast an Arkansas-Rice football game in Houston in the afternoon and then be behind the mike for a special charity game between the Arkansas and Wichita freshman teams in Little Rock the same night. (At the time, freshmen were ineligible for varsity competition and a UA freshman team—the "Shoats"—played a separate schedule against other freshmen teams, usually four or five games per season.)

The Arkansas-Rice game ran longer than usual, and Cheyne's chartered flight back to Little Rock arrived late. Even with a state police escort to War Memorial Stadium, the game was already under way when Cheyne arrived, so his engineer, Harold (Rip) Lindsey, had to announce the opening minutes of the game—and he knew relatively little about football. As Cheyne recalled, when he arrived at the stadium there was no elevator to the press box, so, "I ran up 57 stairs" and was soon able to take over the broadcast. "But I swore I would never, ever, under any circumstances, try to do two ball games in one day."

Another experience Cheyne remembers well involved a game against Ole Miss in Memphis. He arrived in Memphis a couple of days early for his UA sports publicity duties, as was customary for road games, and on game day he asked those who were to work with him on the broadcast to join him for breakfast at the Claridge Hotel in Memphis. When it came time to leave for the stadium, however, his colleagues couldn't find the rental car which had all the broadcast engineering equipment in it. They had parked in the hotel parking garage, but were confused about the exact location of the car. They later learned that the parking lot attendant had moved it to a location more convenient for them, but the group didn't know this. In the meantime, Cheyne said, "I called WMC, one of the largest stations in Memphis, and I told them my plight," and asked if they had an engineer who could help get him on the air at the stadium. The Memphis station was able to help out, and Cheyne went on with the broadcast as scheduled.

Things didn't work out as well for a 1960 basketball game Cheyne thought he broadcast from Baylor University in Waco. It was an exciting, double-overtime game that Arkansas won. After the game, as he often did, he called his wife back in Fayetteville to see how the broadcast had gone. She told him, "The game was not on." Cheyne asked what she meant, and it turned out that one of the lines into the arena had been down and the broadcast was not transmitted back to Arkansas. "I broadcast with all of the excitement I could put in a game—just for myself. That was frustrating. It was a big game for us. We won in overtime," but nobody heard the game. "Only time that ever happened. Thank goodness it wasn't football," he said, noting that the basketball network at the time was relatively small.

Bud Campbell, Frank Broyles, and Growing Interest

By the time that Bud Campbell took over the football and basketball play-by-play responsibilities in 1966, the radio network was solidly established and had 90 stations in eight states, including stations in Poplar Bluff, Missouri, and Shreveport, Louisiana. At the same time, Campbell and the televised *Frank Broyles Show* moved to KATV, Channel 7 in Little Rock. In the years that followed, KATV would build an especially close relationship with Razorback sports and become known as the Razorback station, a point of pride and prestige.

Although new to Arkansas—having attended LSU and previously worked for WIND, a Chicago radio station—Campbell had become one of the state's most familiar faces and voices, beginning with his time as sports director at KARK-TV in 1954, in the early days of television. That also happened to be the year, of course, when interest in Razorback football intensified. Broyles said that a major reason for switching his show to KATV was because of Campbell's move to that station. "I'd always done the show with Bud, who was the most perfect man to work with that I'd ever known," Broyles said.

At that point, *The Frank Broyles Show with Bud Campbell* was generally seen on late Sunday afternoons in the fall. The "live and in color" program featured "color film replays of each Saturday's Arkansas Razorback football game" with analysis by Broyles and Campbell. That was hardly the only TV program focused on the Razorbacks and college football on KATV. In 1968, for example, there was the *NCAA Pre-Game Show* on Saturdays with Campbell and Wilson Matthews, longtime assistant to Broyles and earlier a famed high-school coach at Little Rock Central. On Tuesdays at 10:30 p.m. *Southwest Football Roundup* was seen, with Campbell and legendary sports writer Orville Henry providing commentary. And on Thursday nights at 10:30, Campbell hosted *Arkansas Scouting Report*, with Razorback assistant coaches Mervin Johnson, Cecil "Hootie" Ingram, and Charlie Coffey.

Orville Henry of the *Gazette* was usually invited by Broyles to sit-in off camera while the coach did his TV show. Henry would also use the occasion to pump Broyles for more information about the Razorbacks to be used in his columns and particularly for his lengthy microscopic reviews of the previous week's game, which were eagerly consumed by Razorback fans every Monday morning during football season.

In those days, Broyles and certain other coaches would invite sports journalists to their homes or another gathering place after a game for an informal get-together. Coaches tended to be much more accessible at the time, although these gatherings were not really intended to make news but to enable coaches and writers and broadcasters to get to know each other better. Lou Holtz continued that practice when he succeeded Broyles. And in Austin, University of Texas coach Darrell Royal hosted a similar event after home games at the old Villa Capri Motel near the football stadium.

Part of the reason that Broyles's show, hosted by Campbell and featuring game film and comment from the coach, had such a big following was that there were still very few games carried on television in that era. In the 1966 season, for example, only the Arkansas-Texas game was televised, and that only for a regional audience. In 1967, the UA-UT game was nationally televised, the only national appearance for the Razorbacks that year, coupled with a regional appearance against Texas Tech. National television for the 1967 Texas game was such a big deal that the game program sold at War Memorial Stadium boasted that the game was to be seen on ABC.

As late as the 1988 season, UA had only two regionally televised games and one nationally televised (an 18–16 loss to third-ranked Miami in which eighth-ranked Arkansas almost pulled a major upset). The post-season Cotton Bowl match with UCLA, which featured quarterback Troy Aikman, was also televised nationally.

In 1969, however, the Arkansas-Texas game was definitely on national television and it was a very special event. It also happened to be the 100th anniversary of college football.

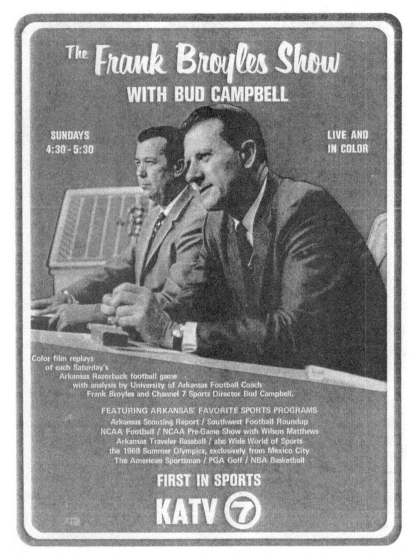

The Frank Broyles Show *was extremely popular with Razorback fans, and Bud Campbell, who hosted the TV show, was the play-by-play radio announcer, 1966– 1974. The program originated from KATV in Little Rock "live and in color."*

UofA Network in its 17th Season

Radio has played an important part in the growth of Razorback football over the last two decades. Now, for the 17th consecutive year, the **UofA Sports Network** will broadcast the entire 10-game schedule of the Porkers to nearly 100 stations in an eight-state area. During the basketball season, the Network follows the complete schedule of the cagers over a 25-station operation. Directing this largest network of its kind in the nation is sports publicity director **Bob Cheyne.**

Play-by-play announcer for the 1968 season will again be **Bud Campbell** of Little Rock, now in his third season with the Porkers. And, providing color commentary will be former Razorback QB **George Walker**, now of Pine Bluff, and **Cheyne.** Network programming has been expanded to include the weekly **Razorback Roundup** program; the new **Ra-** zorback **Report Show** three times a week; and the **Razorback Scoreboard Show** on Saturdays. The UofA Sports Network is a low-cost, non-exclusive (in-state) locally-sponsored operation endorsed by the **Arkansas Broadcaster's Association** with that organization's Board of Directors as advisors. The following list of stations is complete up to publication time. Additional affiliates will be added before the first game.

Station	Freq.	Station	Freq.	Station	Freq.
KVRC, Arkadelphia	1240	KFPW, Fort Smith	1230	KNBY, Newport	1280
KMCW, Augusta	1190	KMAG-FM, Fort Smith	99.1	KXLR, North Little Rock	1150
KSWM, Aurora, Mo.	940	KHOZ, Harrison	900	KOSE, Osceola	860
KWON, Bartlesville, Okla.	1400	KAWW, Heber Springs	1370	KDRS, Paragould	1490
KBTA, Batesville	1340	KFFA, Helena	1360	KCCL, Paris	1460
KBBA, Benton	690	KXAR, Hope	1490	KADL, Pine Bluff	1270
KGKO, Benton	850	KBHS, Hot Springs	590	KPBA, Pine Bluff	1590
KTHS, Berryville	1480	KZNG, Hot Springs	1340	KOTN, Pine Bluff	1490
KLCN, Blytheville	910	KXOW, Hot Springs	1420	KCLA, Pine Bluff	1400
KBRI, Brinkley	1570	KGMR, Jacksonville	1500	KPOC, Pocahontas	1420
KAMD, Camden	910	KBTM, Jonesboro	1230	KLID, Poplar Bluff, Mo.	1340
KJWH, Camden	1450	KNEA, Jonesboro	970	KTPA, Prescott	1370
KDMO, Carthage, Mo.	1490	KODE, Joplin, Mo.	1230	KAMO, Rogers	1390
KLYR, Clarksville	1360	KAAY, Little Rock	1090	KXRJ, Russellville	1490
KCON, Conway	1230	KALO, Little Rock	1250	KWCB, Searcy	1300
KVEE, Conway	1330	KLRA, Little Rock	1010	KRMD, Shreveport, La.	1340
KCCB, Corning	1260	KARK, Little Rock	920	KMPL- Sikeston, Mo.	97.7
KAGH, Crossett	800	KMYO, Little Rock	1050	KUOA, Siloam Springs	1290
KCAB, Dardanelle	980	KVMA, Magnolia	630	KBRS, Springdale	1340
KDQN, DeQueen	1390	KBOK, Malvern	1310	KSPR, Springdale	1590
KDEW, DeWitt	1470	KAMS, Mammoth Spring	1290	KWAK, Stuttgart	1240
KDDA, Dumas	1560	KZOT, Marianna	1460	KTLQ, Tahlequah, Okla.	1350
KDMS, El Dorado	1290	KPCA, Marked Tree	1580	KTFS, Texarkana	1400
KELD, El Dorado	1400	KVSA, McGehee	1220	KOSY, Texarkana	790
KHOG, Fayetteville	1440	WMPS, Memphis, Tenn.	680	KALM, Thayer, Mo.	1290
KFAY, Fayetteville	1250	KENA, Mena	1450	KTMN, Trumann	1530
KFAV, Fayetteville	92.1	KCJC-FM, Merriam, Kan.	98.1	KRMG, Tulsa, Okla.	740
KNWA, Fayetteville	103.9	KNOE,-FM, Monroe, La.	101.9	KRLW, Walnut Ridge	1320
KBJT, Fordyce	1570	KHBM, Monticello	1430	KWRF, Warren	860
KXJK, Forrest City	950	KVOM, Morrilton	800	KSUD, West Memphis	730
KFSA, Fort Smith	950	KTLO, Mountain Home	1240	KWYN, Wynne	1400
KTCS, Fort Smith	1410	KBHC, Nashville	1260		

In the 1968 season, the Razorback network had nearly 100 stations carrying the radio broadcasts. Bob Cheyne remained the network director, with Bud Campbell doing play-by-play "in his third season with the Porkers." There was also other Razorback network programming during football season and a 25-station basketball network for the Razorback "cagers."

There were multiple television and radio programs focusing on Razorback football by 1968, including several on KATV, which featured Razorback assistant coaches and writer Orville Henry, as well as Bud Campbell, the voice of the Razorbacks at the time.

3. The Great Shootout and the 1970s: National Television

The man who conceived of what became known as the "Great Shootout" was Roone Arledge, by that time director of ABC-TV Sports. He became a legendary figure in television. In 1970, Arledge introduced ABC's Monday Night Football, and he was a key figure in popularizing and expanding television sports coverage. He worked on the pioneering *Wide World of Sports* and ten Olympic Games, winning 36 Emmy Awards and becoming the head of ABC News as well.

As recounted by Terry Frei in his book, *Horns, Hogs, & Nixon Coming*, Broyles remembered speaking to Arledge, one of the most powerful broadcasting executives in the country, by phone just before a Razorback Club gathering in "a little gym in Lonoke, Arkansas."

Arledge had a proposal for Broyles and for Darrell Royal, his Texas counterpart: If they would move their 1969 game, scheduled for October 18 that fall in Fayetteville, to December 6, to serve as the regular-season finale in the centennial year of college football, he believed that President Nixon would attend and the game would receive exceptional attention—and, of course, it would be televised on ABC. Arledge had been advised by ABC's college football expert, Beano Cook, that it was likely that Texas and Arkansas would both be undefeated when they met, and that turned out to be the case.

Arledge had also consulted with Bud Wilkinson, ABC's top on-air college football analyst. Wilkinson had been a highly successful coach at Oklahoma. After ending his coaching career, Wilkinson ran for the U.S. Senate in Oklahoma as a Republican in 1964, but lost to Fred Harris. However, Wilkinson was close to Richard Nixon and, after Nixon was elected president in 1968, Wilkinson served as a special consultant to the White House. Broyles said Arledge told him, "Frank, Bud Wilkinson is convinced that you and Texas may be playing for the national championship next season and if you would move the game to December, he'll get President Nixon to come."

Arledge, Wilkinson, and Cook were right about Arkansas and Texas being undefeated heading into their rescheduled December game, and it indeed captured national attention. Texas was ranked number one and Arkansas number two nationally going into the game. Nixon was in Fayetteville for the big game, and many other prominent figures attended. Among them were future President George H. W. Bush, then a Texas congressman, and Jim Wright of Texas, who later became speaker of the U.S. House of Representatives. Arkansas was represented by Governor Winthrop Rockefeller, U.S. Senators J. William Fulbright (a Razorback football star in the 1920s and later UA's president) and John McClellan, and Representative John Paul Hammerschmidt. Henry Kissinger, then Nixon's national security adviser, was also at the game. Evangelist Billy Graham was there and delivered the pre-game invocation.

The ABC telecast featured Chris Schenkel doing play-by-play, with Wilkinson and Bill Fleming also on the broadcast team. Nixon visited the ABC broadcast booth at halftime to discuss the game. Although Razorback Stadium was overflowing on that cold, damp December day, most Arkansas fans were not able to be at the game. Many of them listened to the radio broadcast with Bud Campbell doing the play-by-play—and, as Arkansas fans often do, many turned down the TV volume, preferring to hear the description and comments from the Arkansas broadcast.

Although the game ended disappointingly for Arkansas fans, a heart-breaking 15–14 loss after leading most of the game, the "Great Shootout" ranks as one of the classic college games of all time. The success of that period did enhance Arkansas's national reputation in football, and interest in the Razorbacks within the state continued to escalate. The audience for Razorback sports broadcasts kept growing.

Bud Campbell: A Great Professional

Bud Campbell had begun his ninth season as the football play-by-play announcer in 1974. Just a few days after Arkansas had defeated Tulsa 60–0 in the third game of the 1974 season, however, tragedy struck. Campbell was killed in an automobile accident in Little Rock on October 3, just short of his 51st birthday. As the voice of the Razorbacks and sports director for KATV, Campbell was one of the best-known individuals in the state. His death sent shockwaves across Arkansas, as would the death of Paul Eells 32 years later.

Recalling his work with Campbell on the coach's show, Broyles talked about how easy Campbell was to work with. "He had no ego. He was retiring, and I think he was really a little bit shy off-camera. He was a great professional. He worked harder than any other four people—he did everything. He worked all the time, the same hours as football coaches."

A news director for a rival station in Little Rock, Charles Kelly, who worked at KTHV, later said of Campbell: "He wasn't a classic sportscaster, I mean, a smooth thing, but by golly, he knew the Razorbacks and he worked at it very hard—content-wise he was outstanding."

The widespread familiarity with Campbell and the special place that he and the Razorback broadcasts occupied in Arkansas were evident from comments such as those made by acclaimed fiction writer E. Lynn Harris in 2008. Harris, who in the mid-1970s became the first black cheerleader at the university, later recalled that he originally developed an interest in the Razorbacks "listening to Bud Campbell on a transistor radio and listening to Arkansas games," even though the Razorbacks had no black players when he first began following them. Harris, author of a number of best-selling novels, later returned to the university as an instructor and part-time cheerleading coach before he died in 2009.

Not surprisingly, Larry Foley and Jim Brewer, authors of *Hog Calls*, a 1994 book celebrating 100 years of Razorback football, said in their introduction that they "grew up listening to Bob Cheyne and Bud Campbell describe the exploits of Billy Moore and Lance Alworth, 'Light Horse' Harry Jones and Jon Brittenum." Foley also produced a documentary film, *22 Straight*, which chronicles the Razorbacks' winning streak of 22 games in 1964–65.

Harry King, who spent many years covering Arkansas sports for the Associated Press and then as a columnist for Stephens Media, said, "When I was in college, we'd gather around the radio. We were lucky if we saw the Razorbacks on TV twice a year. When we'd listen to the radio broadcast, we really hung on every word. I guess those were Cheyne's broadcasts. My brother and I would be so wound up at halftime, we'd go outside and throw the football around."

Another who was a regular listener to Razorback football broadcasts as he was growing up was Robert Farrell of Little Rock, who went on to play end for Arkansas, 1976–1979. Farrell has strong memories of listening to those Bud Campbell broadcasts and reading Orville Henry's coverage in the *Gazette*.

Johnson, Woodman, and Smith—and Growing Interest

Following Campbell's death, Fayetteville sports journalist Grant Hall remembered that ABC's Chris Schenkel, the lead TV announcer for college football, came to Arkansas to serve as a temporary replacement for Campbell as the host of the *Frank Broyles Show*.

Television appearances for the Razorbacks were still very limited. In 1974, only the Texas game was televised, and even though the season began with a major intersectional match-up with Southern California in Little Rock, which Arkansas won 22–7, there was no live TV coverage of that game. Interestingly, despite that convincing defeat by the Razorbacks, that USC team wound up ranked number one nationally by United Press International and was considered one of the best teams in Trojans' history.

Bill Johnson stepped in to broadcast the final eight games of the 1974 season on the Arkansas Radio Network. Johnson had previously worked with Campbell as a color commentator or analyst on Razorback broadcasts, and he did some play-by-play announcing when Campbell was doing regional network TV coverage for ABC. Johnson was a busy young man, also doing play-by-play broadcasts for the Conway High School Wampus Cats in his hometown. Johnson began his sports broadcasting career covering Hendrix College basketball games and soon added coverage of what was then Arkansas State Teachers College (later University of Central Arkansas—UCA) football.

As columnist Harry King wrote about Johnson, "For a few years, Johnson was involved with both the Arkansas and UCA broadcasts. He would do an afternoon game in Fayetteville and then do a night game, maybe in Arkadelphia or Searcy. When necessary, he hired Howell Heck to fly him. Whatever the UA gave Johnson for car allowance, he passed on to Heck." Johnson's broadcasting career spanned 46 years as he continued to do UCA football games through 2007.

Dave Cawood, who was then the UA sports information director, sat in with Johnson for the 1974 TCU game, the first after Campbell's death, and then Dave Woodman took on the role of analyst and color commentator. The following year, Woodman became the regular football play-by-play man for the Razorbacks. He had also followed Campbell as the KATV sports anchor in Little Rock. Woodman had previously been working at KARK in Little Rock. "KATV decided that I was the person to replace Bud as the voice of the Razorbacks and to anchor sports at KATV. I accepted the deal." In becoming the sports anchor at KATV and the lead voice of Razorback football, Woodman was following the pattern established by Campbell, which would later be followed by Eells as KATV solidified its place as the Razorback station.

Woodman, whose parents taught at the University of Alabama, began his broadcasting career in Montgomery, Alabama, in 1956, doing a variety of jobs at a television station and radio play-by-play for high school football. He next moved to KNOE-TV in Monroe, Louisiana, a station that also had viewers in southern Arkansas. Again, he added radio play-by-play for high school sports and also became the radio announcer for

Northeast Louisiana (later University of Louisiana–Monroe) football and basketball. When the TV station added a sportscast to its 10 p.m. news program, Woodman was given a chance to do the nightly sports report. Woodman spent 13 years at the Monroe station (1957–1970), playing many different roles. After leaving television briefly, he moved on to KTVE-TV in El Dorado for a short stint and then was hired by KARK-TV in Little Rock, where he became the station's sports anchor.

Woodman made the move from KARK to KATV to succeed Campbell as the station's sports anchor. "I was at KATV from 1974–1977, anchoring the sports at 6 o'clock and 10 o'clock and broadcasting University of Arkansas football and basketball games on radio," he said. He was the broadcaster during the highly successful 1975 football season when the Razorbacks were SWC co-champions and defeated Georgia 31–10 in the Sugar Bowl. And he was the voice of the Razorbacks during Broyles's final season as coach in 1976.

Broadcasting Arkansas basketball during those years was a highlight for Woodman. "I began the same year Eddie Sutton took over as head basketball coach," Woodman later told Tommy Booras for his study of pioneering TV sportscasters. Woodman recalled that when he began broadcasting Razorback basketball games, "the southwest corner of Barnhill Arena was nothing but dirt and sawdust." He described for Arkansas fans the building of basketball success under Sutton. By 1976–77, Sutton guided the Razorbacks to a 28–2 season and an NCAA tournament bid with a team led by Sidney Moncrief, Marvin Delph, and Ron Brewer—the "Triplets."

"I got to see them in all their glory," Woodman said. "I got close to the athletes. I identified with them," he told Joe Stumpe for a profile in the *Arkansas Democrat-Gazette*. "I was probably overly enthusiastic. Those were the sawdust days at Barnhill. I loved every minute of it."

However, as Woodman told Booras, "I was notified by Athletic Director Frank Broyles in March 1977 that I would be replaced at the end of basketball season. I was never told why, officially, by anyone."

The Razorback broadcast job wasn't all that Woodman lost. "It wasn't written down anywhere, but it was generally accepted that the play-by-play voice for Arkansas also did sports at KATV...it was two jobs and two checks for one hire. Anyone who did play-by-play for the University of Arkansas also anchored sports at Channel 7 (KATV). When I lost the play-by-play job, I also lost the job at Channel 7. Basketball season ended about two weeks after I was notified by Frank, and I was out of two jobs.... I had to start over again."

Woodman did start over again, working in both advertising and television—and eventually he went back to KARK (Channel 4) and became that station's sports director and anchor for a time. In that job, he was involved in coverage of Razorback sports during the era when Lou Holtz and Ken Hatfield coached the football Hogs. Because of the great interest in the Razorbacks and the competition with KATV, KARK devoted significant resources to covering the Razorbacks. "I went with a photographer and went to Holtz's hometown of East Liverpool, Ohio, and interviewed people he had grown up with, people he went to school with, that sort of thing. Later, we sent a crew to Los Angeles and did a feature on Holtz when he was a guest on the *Tonight Show*. We spent all sorts of money on that special program, but money was no object." (It was on that appearance on NBC's *Tonight* when Holtz, asked if Fayetteville was at the end of the world, said, "No, but you can see it from there."

He was known for his clever quips, but that comment earned him the ire of some in Arkansas.)

The 1977 football season, with Holtz as coach, was a highly successful one for the Razorbacks, marred only by a 13–9 loss to Texas in a nationally televised game. At the end of the season, Arkansas was matched against Oklahoma, ranked second nationally, in the Orange Bowl. Although they were 18-point underdogs, the Razorbacks trounced the Sooners 31–6 in one of the biggest upsets in school history. As the *New York Times* reported, "While more than 15,000 Arkansas travelers in a crowd of 68,500 bellowed for their beloved Hogs, the Razorbacks dominated college football's top rushing team." For those Arkansas fans who weren't among the 15,000 at the game, it was televised nationally on NBC in addition to being carried on the Razorback radio network.

Woodman was succeeded in the Razorback broadcasting booth and at KATV that year by Sam Smith, who handled the Razorback announcing responsibilities for just one year, then left to become the play-by-play announcer for the San Antonio Spurs of the National Basketball Association. Smith spent 25 years calling NBA games for the Spurs, Miami Heat, Charlotte Hornets, and Charlotte Bobcats, and also worked for ESPN covering a variety of sports.

Follow Arkansas Football on Radio

Follow the Razorbacks with Dave Woodman and Mike Nail on these fine Arkansas Radio Stations.:

DAVE WOODMAN
PLAY BY PLAY

MIKE NAIL
COLOR

STATION	LOCATION	STATION	LOCATION
KVRC AM	Arkadelphia	KFIN FM	Jonesboro
KMLA FM	Ashdown	KUUZ FM	Lake Village
KMCW/KABK FM	Augusta	KAAY	Little Rock
KBTA	Batesville	KARN AM	Little Rock
KSCC FM	Berryville	KLRA AM	Little Rock
KJON FM	Booneville	KVMA/KFMV	Magnolia
KBRI/KBRI FM	Brinkley	KBOK AM	Malvern
KFCM FM	Cherokee Village (Hardy)	KENA	Mena
KGFL/KHPQ	Clinton	KHBM/KHBM FM	Monticello
KCON AM	Conway	KVOM/KVOM FM	Morrilton
KDQN FM	DeQueen	KTLO	Mountain Home
KDEW/KDEW FM	DeWitt	KWOZ FM	Mountain View (Batesville)
KDMS/KLBQ	El Dorado	KJKK FM	Murfreesboro
KELD/KAYZ	El Dorado	KNAS FM	Nashville
KELC AM	England	KZRK FM	Ozark
KNWA FM	Fayetteville	KDRS AM	Paragould
KBJT AM	Fordyce	KHIG FM	Paragould
KXJK/KBFC FM	Forrest City	KARV AM	Russellville
KFSA AM	Fort Smith	KSAR FM	Salem
KTCS/KTCS FM	Fort Smith	KWCK/KSER	Searcy
KWXI AM	Glenwood	KMSL FM	Stamps
KHOZ FM	Harrison	KOSY	Texarkana
KAWW/KAWW FM	Heber Springs	KRWA FM	Waldron
KCRI/KCRI FM	Helena	KWRF AM/FM	Warren
KFFA AM	Helena	KCTT AM	Yellville
KHPA AM	Hope		
KXAR AM	Hope		
KACQ	Hot Springs		
KBHS/KSPA	Hot Springs		
KZNG/KWBO	Hot Springs		

HOW BOUT DEM HOGS!!

Southwest Conference Radio Network

A BROADCAST DIVISION OF HOST COMMUNICATIONS, INC.

For the 1983 season, Dave Woodman and Mike Nail handled Arkansas football radio broadcasts while the Razorback games were part of the Southwest Conference network. Nail was also the longtime voice of Razorback basketball.

Bud Campbell
Voice of the Razorbacks

Paul Eells
Voice of the Razorbacks

Though neither had Arkansas roots, Bud Campbell and Paul Eells became two of the state's best-known citizens during their years as voices of the Razorbacks.

4. Into the 1980s and the Paul Eells Era

Sam Smith's successor as the voice of the Razorbacks was to become a beloved and widely known figure. Before his shocking death in an auto accident in 2006, Paul Eells had served nearly 30 years as the distinctive voice of the Razorbacks.

When he took the job in 1978, he had no previous connection with Arkansas. An Iowa native and University of Iowa graduate, Eells was working in Nashville when he was hired by KATV and the Razorback network. He had spent ten years in Nashville as sports director at WSM-TV and play-by-play radio announcer for Vanderbilt football and basketball. Previously, he had worked at a smaller station in Cedar Rapids, Iowa, where he covered a lot of high school sports and got a chance to do some play-by-play on radio for University of Iowa football and basketball.

"Nashville was a much larger city, and I was exposed to a much larger audience there," Eells told Tommy Booras. However, he said there was something different about working in the Tennessee capital. "There wasn't much of a commitment to sports in Nashville," Eells said. (That was long before Nashville had an NFL franchise, the Tennessee Titans.) "In fact, the station I worked at in Cedar Rapids was more committed to sports than WSM was. Because

WSM owned the rights to and broadcast the Grand Ole Opry, the station was more interested in that than in sports. County-and-western music was WSM's number-one priority."

When he was contacted by Athletic Director Broyles in 1978 about doing play-by-play for the Razorbacks, he found out that the job also involved being the sports anchor for KATV in Little Rock, with its strong commitment to Razorback sports. "It was two jobs in one. I remember going to Fayetteville and meeting Broyles, foot-ball Coach Lou Holtz, and basketball Coach Eddie Sutton. I had to have their approval before anything could happen."

Although a newcomer to Arkansas, within a few years Eells had endeared himself to Razorback fans and became an iconic figure in the state. As sports director at KATV, which could be seen in many parts of the state through cable television, he was recognized everywhere he went. In addition to his play-by-play radio broadcasts of Razorback football, he also did TV play-by-play for a selection of Razorback basketball games carried by the Razorback Sports Network and was the host for the TV football and basketball coaches shows.

Razorback fans came to treasure his signature calls: "Oh My!" and "Touchdown Arkansas!" Those trademark words in Eells's familiar voice are associated with especially memorable moments in Razorback history such as the "Miracle on Markham" 21–20 last-minute victory in Little Rock over LSU in 2002; the 58–56 win over Ole Miss in 2001 in seven overtimes with its repeated do-or-die moments; or the 28–24 triumph over Tennessee in Fayetteville in 1999 after the heart-breaking loss to the then-number-one-ranked Vols at Knoxville in 1998. It was Eells who described those high and low points to Arkansas fans. For his part, Eells cited Arkansas's 2000 Cotton Bowl victory over Texas as one of his favorites among many memorable games that he broadcast, and, of course, the nail-biting seven-overtime Razorback win at Ole Miss in 2001, with 114 total points scored, nine lead changes, and 988 yards of combined offense. The seven-overtime victory over Kentucky in 2003 ranked high on his list as well.

Radio sports shows in Arkansas still regularly replay some of the more memorable moments of Eells describing the Razorbacks in action. Listening to those recordings "still gives me goose-bumps" said Tommy Craft, a Fort Smith sports talk-show host. Randy Rainwater, who has a statewide radio sports show, says he never gets tired of listening to those replays.

Liz Beadle of Little Rock, who entered the University of Arkansas as a student in 2010, said some of her strongest childhood memories are of listening to Razorback games on the radio. "I was one of the few eight year olds on the planet with the attention span to listen to a three-and-a-half-hour college football game on the radio. As an infant, I must have known Paul Eells's voice as well as I knew my parents' voices."

"Paul was the one who made it acceptable to turn the sound down on the television and listen to ARSN broadcasts on the radio," said veteran sports journalist Grant Hall. "Losses were just easier to accept with his kinder, more gentle approach to play-by-play. Understand, what you saw and heard with Paul is what you got."

Being the voice of the Razorbacks is a title in Arkansas only a little less significant than head coach and slightly more elevated than governor, the *Arkansas Democrat-Gazette* said in an editorial after Eells died.

Eells was known for his modesty and humility, his willingness to talk with any Razorback fan he encountered, and for being an all-around good guy. He was a connecting point for Razorback followers around the state and beyond.

In 1993, he told Booras, "I'm happy with what I've been able to do. I am unhappy that I don't think I've become as good as I think I could be. I would love to spend more time working on my play-by-play skills. I wish I had the time to be in Fayetteville more and watch film with the football coaches and get to know the players better." However, he added, "I wouldn't change a thing about my career. I've been able to travel all over the country and meet lots of people. I feel truly blessed."

In fact, through the years, Eells worked hard to stay informed about all aspects of Razorback sports and to be well acquainted with coaches and players. And listeners thought his play-by-play skills were top notch. Eells's work in Arkansas included 19 football bowl games as the play-by-play voice and 52 NCAA Tournament basketball games as either the radio voice of the Razorbacks or reporting for KATV.

In 2006, at age 70, he was preparing for his 29th season as the UA football radio play-by-play announcer. He had told friends that the upcoming season might be his last before retiring, though those who knew him well thought it would be hard for him to step away completely. He also hosted the football and basketball coaches' shows in addition to his duties as sports director at KATV.

Eells had made the Fayetteville-to-Little Rock drive dozens of times under all sorts of conditions. On July 31, 2006, he had played in Coach Houston Nutt's golf tournament at Stonebridge Meadows Golf Club in Fayetteville and had done his final sportscast for KATV from the golf course. On the drive back to Little Rock, his car crossed the median line on I-40 near Russellville and hit a car driven by Billie J. Burton of Dover, killing both of them.

News of Eells's death spread quickly, with TV stations reporting the story later that evening and extensive newspaper coverage the following day. Steve Sullivan, KATV's lead sports anchor, had spoken to Eells by phone shortly before his death. He learned of the accident involving his friend and mentor right before going on the air with the 10 p.m. newscast. Until the station was able to confirm the news and verify that Eells's family has been notified, the staff held off reporting the story until later that night. "It was really tough," said Sullivan. "You usually want to be excited when you're talking about sports, and you couldn't be excited. But Paul was an ultimate professional, and we had to get through it."

At rival station KARK, news director Rob Heverling said, "We learned of it right around 10 p.m., but we wanted to let Channel 7 lead with it, not just out of respect for Paul but out of respect for Channel 7."

The following day, KATV anchors Scott Inman and Christina Munoz and meteorologist Barry Brandt broke down when talking about Eells during the 5 p.m. newscast. Sullivan said, "My dad passed about eight years ago, and Paul was like another dad to me. He was like that to a lot of people. The guy never had bad days. He enjoyed himself right up to the last minute. He was still on top of his game. He looked good, he sounded good. I think he could have kept going as long as the team was winning."

Steve Barnes, longtime Little Rock newsman, worked with both Campbell and Eells and said both were easy to work with and were true professionals who enjoyed what they did and had the respect of all their colleagues.

Another great SEC broadcaster, Larry Munson, who broadcast Georgia football games for more than 40 years, told Scott Cain of the Democrat-Gazette, "When I left Vanderbilt to come to Atlanta to do the Braves and Georgia, he took my job at WSM in Nashville. He was a very good guy, nice to be around, and super, super friendly. And a hell of a radio man. It's just a terrible tragedy."

Jimmy Dykes, who worked 12 years with Eells on televised Razorback basketball games, said he learned from Eells how important it is to know the name of not only the broadcast producers but everybody involved in the broadcast. Eells was known for treating everyone equally well.

Harry King underlined this point, recalling that he and Eells were playing a golf tournament in Pine Bluff and got there early to hit some balls. "He gets on the putting green and it was like a process. 'Paul, I'm so-and-so from Star City. Remember that Ole Miss game?' Or 'I'm so-and so from wherever. Remember the LSU game when Matt Jones got loose?' I'm ready to hit balls and I'm saying, 'Paul, come on.' But it was important to him. It was important to accommodate people." King added, "We've been to the McDonald's in Clarksville and people will ask for his autograph and you think, 'How much can the guy do?'"

"He never comprehended that he was so big. In this business there are some people with some egos, but he had none," King said. He also said that Eells was "one of the hardest-working guys around," noting that when he was hosting *The Nolan Richardson Show*, he would sometimes drive to the airport in Fayetteville late at night to meet Coach Richardson when he got off the plane after a road game. "Even when a team got beat, he made it sound good, like everything was okay, and that's a real skill."

Keith Jackson, the former Oklahoma and NFL star who was the analyst alongside Eells for six seasons of Razorback broadcasts, told Scott Cain of the *Democrat-Gazette*, "It'll be tough when Arkansas scores its first touchdown and I'm listening for 'Touchdown Arkansas!' and waiting for that 'Oh, my,' and it's not there."

"He was the heartbeat of sports in the state of Arkansas, and his kindness, his character, and his wonderful voice will remain with all of us who knew him, or loved sports because of him," said Jerry Jones, owner of the Dallas Cowboys and former Razorback.

Mike Huckabee, governor of Arkansas at the time of Eells's death, said, "He gave us far more than news about sports, but gave the people of Arkansas his spirit of contagious joy. In a highly competitive sportscasting business, he stood alone as a tower of statesmanship and sportsmanship in both his professional and personal life."

When he learned of Eells's death, Frank Broyles said, "The Razorback family has lost a tremendous ambassador with the passing of Paul Eells. He was the consummate professional and always represented the state and the Razorbacks with the utmost class."

"He was the voice that represented the state," said Houston Nutt, the Razorbacks' football coach at the time Eells died. "It was a very defined voice. It was a gift he had. People related to that and there was an immediate connection, a bond."

At the Arkansas football season opener in September 2006, there were special tributes to Eells. At halftime of the game with Southern California, the Arkansas band spelled out PAUL EELLS and then moved into a "Touchdown Arkansas" formation. Before the game, the giant screen above the Broyles Athletic Complex showed a video tribute to Eells, concluding with his call of the Clint Stoerner to Anthony Lucas touchdown pass that resulted in a win over Tennessee in 1999.

In the press box, Kevin Trainor and the UA sports information staff had a handout at each seat in memory of Eells and his career, and of J. E. Dunlap, who covered the Razorbacks for more than 60 years for the *Harrison Daily Times*.

Eells voice lives on through repeated broadcasts of famous moments in the Razorbacks' history that he described. "Paul's calls" are treasured by Arkansas fans.

In 2012, on the sixth anniversary of Eells's death, Ched Carpenter, who hosts a sports-talk radio show on 1190 "The Fan" in Fayetteville, played some of Eells's most memorable calls. Carpenter said that even though he didn't personally know Eells, "Losing Paul was like losing a member of your family, like losing your favorite uncle."

Paul Eells was an Arkansas classic, and his broadcast calls of notable moments in Razorback games are still treasured by fans.

Some of the best-remembered of Paul's classic calls:

Touchdown Arkansas...Lucas goes up...makes the catch—23 yards, and the Razorbacks have the lead.

Fayetteville, November 13, 1999: Arkansas 28, Tennessee 24, ending Tennessee's hopes of a second straight national championship after Arkansas had dropped a heart-breaking loss to the Vols the previous year. Anthony Lucas caught Clint Stoerner's pass for the winning score. Arkansas fans stormed the field after the game and for the first time since 1981, the goal posts came down.

There's the snap, Jones looking, Jones now...throwing to the end zone...and it issssss COMPLETE—TOUCHDOWN! Oh my! I can't believe it—31 yards to DeCori Birmingham in the back of the end zone, and this game is tied at 20–20.

Little Rock, November 29, 2002 (The "Miracle on Markham"): Arkansas 21, LSU 20. This call has been replayed often on Arkansas sports shows. A voice other than Eells's can be heard excitedly cheering in the background. Some years later, Rick Schaeffer said that Chuck Barrett had acknowledged that the other voice was his.

Jones at the 40, Jones at the 30, Jones at the 20, Jones—and he is out of bounds at about the 12 on a terrific run by the young freshman, 37 yards.

November 3, 2001: Freshman Matt Jones came off the bench to rush for 110 yards and two scores, completed three of six passes for 61 yards and another score, and threw for two two-point conversions during overtime periods to lead Arkansas to a seven-overtime 58–56 victory over Ole Miss.

58-56, [Eli] Manning awaiting the snap…Manning rolling out, going over the middle…it is…Arkansas wins! Arkansas wins! The two-point conversion falls short, despite the pass being complete, and the Hogs race on the field— in the longest overtime game in the history of 1-A college football.

Oxford, 2001: Razorback linebacker Jermaine Petty tackled Rebel receiver Doug Zeigler at the two yard line, ending the thrilling win over Ole Miss.

Matt Jones back in and Pierce and Cobbs are in the I-formation. Pierce the fullback at the bottom of the I. The give to Cobbs, right up the middle…Cobbs at the 40, Cobbs at the 30, Cobbs at the 20, Cobbs at the 10. Touchdown Arkansas!

Austin, September 13, 2003: Cedric Cobbs puts the Hogs ahead of Texas 28–14.

There's a fumble, and the Hogs come up with it….That's it! The ball game is over! Lorenzen was stopped short of the first down and lost the football and the Hogs came up with it, and in seven overtimes in Lexington, Kentucky, Arkansas will go home finally with a smile on its face, 71–63.

Lexington, November 1, 2003: The seven-overtime 71–63 win over Kentucky.

Johnson up under center—handoff…at the 30, 35, 40, midfield, Georgia 40, McFadden at the 30, the 20, the 10—Touchdown Arkansas!

October 22, 2005: Freshman Darren McFadden rushed for 190 yards against fourth-ranked Georgia, an indication of what was to come in his fabled career.

Coach Nolan Richardson, who guided Arkansas basketball (1985–2002) to some great seasons was often interviewed by Paul Eells before and after Razorback games.

Paul Eells and Frank Broyles became Arkansas institutions. Broyles coached the Razorbacks 19 seasons, with 144 wins, seven SWC championships, and a national championship in1964. He also served as athletic director from 1973 to 2008. Eells was the primary voice of the Razorbacks from 1978 to 2006, and almost all Razorback fans regarded him as a friend.

In addition to play-by-play of Razorback games, Paul Eells hosted shows for UA football and basketball coaches including Nolan Richardson, coach of the 1994 basketball national champions.

Winning national championship honors in basketball in 1993–94 generated great excitement among Razorback fans, and Paul Eells, who won many broadcasting honors, helped build that excitement. However, the schedule of televised games involving SEC teams for the 1994–95 season (when Arkansas returned to the championship game) shows far fewer TV games than would be televised in subsequent years.

The Lou Holtz Show

Head Coach Lou Holtz and KATV Sports Director Paul Eells
review last week's Razorback game, preview the upcoming
game and interview the players. Thursday nights at 10:30.

EXCLUSIVELY ON SUPERSEVEN

*The weekly coach's show during football season was seen on Sunday afternoon for
many years but later moved to different times. In 1982, Coach Lou Holtz and
Paul Eells were seen on Thursday nights at 10:30.*

A media ID badge identified Paul Eells, who was sports director at KATV in addition to his Razorback broadcasting role, but he needed no ID—he was recognized everywhere he went in Arkansas.

5. Into the 1990s: Mike Nail Steps In

After Eells died, Mike Nail was asked to take on the football play-by-play responsibilities on an interim basis. Nail had been handling the radio play-by-play for basketball since 1981–82 and was a major figure in Razorback sports broadcasting until his retirement in 2010. The affable Nail was at the microphone for nearly 940 Arkansas basketball games, including one of the paramount moments in Razorback sports history. *"Arkansas wins the national championship!"* he shouted excitedly from the 1994 NCAA basketball championship game in Charlotte, North Carolina, as Arkansas defeated Duke for the national title.

When Broyles approached Nail about taking the football announcing job for the 2007 season, it was an "emotional, tense, and challenging time for me," he said. "I'm very happy doing the games, very thankful. And more than that, I'm very humbled to be occupying the space that Paul occupied so brilliantly."

"When you listen to somebody for 28 years and you're around them for 28 years, they're going to influence your style some and you're going to influence their style some," Nail told Cyd King of the *Arkansas Democrat-Gazette* in November 2006. "It concerned me for a long time that I would say something or do something that would impinge upon Paul's style and way of doing things. I really had to think about that a lot and worried about it a lot."

Nail was nearing the end of a long career in radio and television and close association with Arkansas sports, but he was a perfect choice to step in after Eells's death. Nail was especially well suited to play a transitional role in the football broadcasts, because he was well known and a familiar voice to most Razorback fans as the longtime basketball broadcaster. He also had done color analysis for football from 1978 to 1990.

Nail had only a few weeks to prepare for the 2006 football season and the first game against Southern California. He spent long hours researching players and statistics and updating his knowledge of football rules. "You've got to study the other team, too," said Nail, noting, for example, that he wouldn't have wanted to broadcast the USC game without noting that Trojan quarterback John David Booty's father once was a quarterback at Arkansas. Nail developed his own spotting boards for the games with the help of computer programs, cardboard backing, and a yellow highlighter pen.

His season doing football play-by-play was a highly successful one for Arkansas. That 2006 team won the SEC western division championship and ended with a 10–4 record, including wins over Alabama (in overtime), Auburn, and Tennessee and featuring such stars as Darren McFadden, Felix Jones, Peyton Hillis, Jonathan Luigs, Chris Houston, and Jamaal Anderson.

There were some hectic days when the 2006 basketball season began and football was still underway. Nail called the basketball season opener, an exhibition game with Xavier. Three days later, he was in South Carolina to call the football team's nail-biter victory over the Gamecocks. Arriving back in Fayetteville late that night, he was on the job the next morning for the taping of *The*

Houston Nutt Show. In between two more home basketball games the next week, he prepared for the football Hogs' last Fayetteville game, a critical contest against Tennessee. Except for a slight slip of the tongue when he mistakenly said that Arkansas running back Felix Jones "fumbled the basketball," Nail appeared to have no problem keeping it all straight. He continued moving back and forth between the two sports for the remainder of November, including a trip to Orlando, Florida, for a basketball tournament immediately after the football team ended its regular season against LSU. "It's a juggling act," Nail said to Cyd King. "But it's not difficult to switch from one to the other because I've been around it all my life, and it's something I really enjoy."

Nail continued as the basketball announcer through the 2009-2010 season. Being a sports announcer for the Razorbacks was "a dream come true," Nail, who grew up in Fayetteville, told Tommy Booras. "I always wanted to broadcast Arkansas games. I listened to Bob Cheyne as a youngster...I idolized him." As Nail neared the end of his career, Cheyne said Nail had a style of his own. "Mike's got a good personality, and he's very knowledgeable about sports. He's trained his mind to keep his eye on the action on the field."

Nail: Fulfilling a Dream

Mike Nail said he used to lock himself in his room with an old tape recorder and make up his own games as he went along. "I remember becoming interested in sports broadcasting when I was 12 or 13. I remember the 'Falstaff Game of the Week,' with Dizzy Dean and Buddy Blatner and Pee Wee Reese. I remember watching the 1956 World Series on television when Don Larson of the Yankees pitched the only perfect game in World Series history. Those things got me thinking about sports broadcasting as a career."

Nail began his career in sports journalism in 1963 working for the *Northwest Arkansas Times* as a sports writer. His first television job was in Conway at what became the Arkansas Educational Television Network (AETN). By 1969, he was working at KATV in Little Rock, where he produced sportscasts for Bud Campbell. He then moved to KFSM-TV in Fort Smith as sports director in 1971. He remembers that sports coverage on the station in those early days often lacked film footage. "Typically, a reporter would go out on a story assignment with a Polaroid camera, shoot a still picture for the story, bring it back to the station, tape the photograph on an easel in the studio, and shoot the photo with a studio camera."

However, Nail was determined to get involved in coverage of Razorback sports as well. "Razorback sports were huge events and we had to cover them. I used to go up to Fayetteville once or twice a week. Football was the big sport but basketball was just starting to gain interest among fans. When Lanny Van Eman became the head basketball coach (1970–71), things started to happen with that program. He was the first coach to use the term 'Running Razorbacks.' I saw that fan support was beginning to build, so I worked on the management of KFSM to produce a basketball show. KATV had a football show with Frank Broyles locked up, but no one was doing basketball, so I thought we should jump on that." However, KFSM management wasn't enthusiastic about producing a basketball show, and Nail really had to fight to get it on the air. As Nail remembers, "The station would rent a plane, fly it to Fayetteville and pick up the coach, and fly him back to Fort Smith where someone would pick him up at the airport and drive him to the station. We'd tape the show, drive him back to the airport, and fly him to Fayetteville. That went on every week."

From Fort Smith, Nail's career took him to Joplin, Missouri, and Oklahoma City, and he gained valuable experience as a sportscaster at KWTV in Oklahoma City and on radio broadcasts of minor league baseball. In 1978, he returned to Northwest Arkansas and became an established figure in covering Arkansas sports. In addition to being involved in covering the Razorbacks, Nail had stints as sports anchor for two TV stations in Northwest Arkansas.

Nail decided he would retire from regular broadcasting duties after the 2009–10 season. "I will forever be grateful to Frank Broyles, then-athletic director, and Eddie Sutton, then the Arkansas head coach, for giving me the opportunity to realize one of my life's dreams, which was inspired by my longtime friend Bob Cheyne, former Arkansas sports information director and the 'Voice of the Razorbacks' for many years," Nail told *Inside Razorback Athletics* at the time of his retirement.

Nail broadcast Razorback roundball during the final years (1982–1985) of Sutton's time at Arkansas then continued throughout the time of Nolan Richardson's coaching tenure (1986–2002) and the years of Stan Heath (2003–2007), and concluded with three years with John Pelphrey as coach. Nail's time broadcasting Razorback basketball included the 1994 national championship, three trips to the Final Four, 17 NCAA tournaments, two NIT appearances, and eight conference championships.

The final seconds and the conclusion of the Arkansas win over Duke in the championship game in 1994 will be long remembered in Razorback lore.

As Nail described the shot that determined the outcome:

Right side…Thurman…He's open for three—Good!

Seconds later, Nail had the satisfaction of shouting to his radio audience:

Arkansas wins the national championship! The Arkansas Razorbacks have completed a dream season.

Asked later by Matt Turner of KNWA if he had planned what he would say if Arkansas won, Nail said he had no idea beforehand what he might say at that moment of victory for Arkansas. He remembered that he was nervous before the game got underway, but once it did, everything settled down. Nail said that what was notable about the 1994 champions was that "they played as a team, each player knew exactly what his role was."

While that basketball national championship was the obvious highlight of Nail's time as the Razorbacks' broadcaster, he remembers many great games. "There have been just so many memorable games that I could go just on and on and still leave a lot of them out. But, there have been a lot of great games with Kentucky and Tennessee when they were really good. Unlike the Southwest Conference, in which Arkansas, Texas, and Houston dominated, the competitive nature is more balanced in the SEC, so there have been some great, great games."

One game that stands out in Nail's memory wasn't a conference game but the 1991 high-profile matchup with UNLV, ranked number one at the time, with Arkansas ranked second nationally. "We were still playing at Barnhill Fieldhouse [Arena] at the time. Students camped out for days and days. It was just a great, great atmosphere. The game was nationally televised, and it just a great game, although UNLV won 112–105."

Another he recalls vividly was a game played in Pine Bluff in 1984. For several years during that era, Arkansas scheduled a non-conference game at the Pine Bluff Convention Center.

On February 11, 1984, Arkansas had played in Dallas and beaten SMU. The team was supposed to fly to Pine Bluff after that game for the next day's game against North Carolina, 19–0 at the time and ranked number one nationally. However, as Nail remembers, tornadic weather prevented the team from leaving Dallas Saturday night. "So we had to wait until the next day. Players dressed in their uniforms and sweats in Dallas and flew to Pine Bluff in one of the roughest flights I've ever been on. Several players got sick. We went straight to the Pine Bluff Convention Center and played and beat number-one North Carolina on a last-second shot by Charles Balentine." As Nail points out, Michael Jordan was the leading scorer for the Tarheels in that game, with 21 points, on a team that also featured Sam Perkins and Brad Daugherty. Arkansas was led by Joe Kleine, who scored 20 in the 65–64 win.

"I started broadcasting at Arkansas the year after Sidney Moncrief's last year," Nail said, but he saw many great players perform for the Razorbacks. "Joe Kleine and Alvin Robertson were on the 1984 Olympic team and won gold medals that year. Tony Brown went on to play in the NBA. Darrell Walker played and coached in the NBA. Then there were all the great players—Corliss Williamson and Scotty Thurman from the 1994 team, and earlier Todd Day, Lee Mayberry, Oliver Miller, and Andrew Lang. There was Dwight Stewart, Cory Beck, Joe Johnson—who signed a $70 million contract with the Atlanta Hawks. More recently there was Ronnie Brewer. There have just been so many great players."

On senior day 2010, with Arkansas playing Ole Miss in the home finale of the season, Nail was honored at a halftime ceremony, and those in attendance received a Mike Nail talking bobblehead that had the recorded call of the final moment from that 1994 national championship season.

Commenting on Nail, Broyles told sports writer Nate Allen that he describes a game without taking over the game while keeping Arkansas fans in the game. "You don't stay on the job as long as he did," Broyles said, "unless you are accepted by the fans. They recognize his voice immediately and they recognize he is a Razorback. He described the game to the point they didn't just listen, they were emotionally involved. There are not many who can do that without talking too much, but Mike brings that. He described the game and the emotion that goes with it."

Nail said of his years doing basketball, "We did things to try to make our broadcast better every year," noting the addition of pre-game and post-game shows and interviews with the coach.

"Mike is a perfect example of a person whose dreams came true," said Rick Schaeffer, who worked with Nail on the air for all but four of those years of basketball broadcasts. "He grew up in Fayetteville with the goal of one day becoming the 'Voice of the Razorbacks.' It's one thing to achieve your dream; it's another to live it as long as Mike has. Twenty-nine years in broadcasting is nearly an eternity."

Rick Schaeffer: Arkansas Sports Authority

Rick Schaeffer had a distinctive perspective, having been in-volved with Arkansas sports broadcasting in a variety of capacities since he joined the UA sports information staff in 1976 and served as sports information director from 1979 to 2000. Even after leaving that post he continued to be involved in broadcasts of basketball, football, and baseball. In the process, Schaeffer be-came known as an authority on the history of Razorback sports. In addition to other roles, he has long experience as a co-host of radio and television call-in and talk shows devoted primarily to the Razorbacks. For 12 years, Schaeffer and Grant Hall, another longtime observer of Arkansas sports, had a weekly radio show in Northwest Arkansas, and then a TV program. Later, Schaeffer joined with Randy Rainwater in hosting a popular statewide radio show heard every weekday afternoon.

Not surprisingly, the national championship in basketball in 1994 ranks as a highlight of Schaeffer's career with Razorback sports. Although he grew up in Oklahoma and graduated from Oklahoma State University, Schaeffer was a Razorback fan and listened to his first Razorback football games on KAAY ("The Mighty 1090"), a Little Rock station that at the time broadcast with a 50,000-watt signal that could be heard in much of mid-America.

Working with Eells and Nail on Razorback broadcasts was a privilege, Schaeffer said. "It's a good feeling. You feel like you're gathering with the family on game day. Paul Eells was great....To be able to work with Paul Eells was wonderful. He was a phenomenal person and superb broadcaster. Really, it's just knowing people out there listening want the same thing you want. They want the Razorbacks to win and they want you to describe it to them." Schaeffer noted that he and Nail worked together so long "that we almost know what each other will say before we say it."

Schaeffer has had the opportunity to cover or work with many great Razorback athletes. Among those he remembers most strongly are basketball stars Sidney Moncrief, Lee Mayberry, and Scotty Thurman. He said Moncrief was "a rare and special human being. He was a leader and was just special. He and Mayberry had that great combination of ability and humility." Among the football standouts he particularly enjoyed working with were Quinn Grovey, Billy Ray Smith Jr., Brad Taylor, and Anthony Lucas.

He understandably ranks being in on the broadcast of the 1994 national championship in basketball as a career high point and emphasizes that the Razorbacks went back to the championship game again the following year. "Not many people get to do that. It was a rare privilege."

He also vividly remembers when U. S. Reed sank a half-court shot to beat Louisville 74–73 in the NCAA tournament in 1981. "That's one of the few times I remember coming out of my seat," the broadcaster said. A top football highlight was when Arkansas beat Texas in the Cotton Bowl in 2000, Schaeffer's last game as football color analyst.

In addition to Eells and Nail, Schaeffer also has good memories of working with Sam Smith and Dave Woodman on Razorback broadcasts. And he came to know well journalists covering the Razorbacks, including Orville Henry, radio's Jim Elder, and Bill Connors, longtime sports editor at the *Tulsa World*. From the national networks, Schaeffer enjoyed getting to know broadcasters such as Jim Nantz of CBS and Keith Jackson of ABC. And he was influenced in his own career by baseball announcers Harry Caray and Jack Buck. (Though best known for baseball, both Caray and Buck also did football play-by-play. Interestingly, Caray, famous for his coverage of baseball's St. Louis Cardinals and Chicago Cubs, was the announcer for national radio network coverage of the Cotton Bowl game when Arkansas played in the Dallas classic in 1966. And Bob Cheyne remembers that Caray did the Missouri football radio broadcast when the Tigers played Arkansas in Little Rock in 1963.)

Behind the Scenes

While the voices of the Razorbacks—those actually doing play-by-play and broadcast commentary—become well known to Hog fans, there are, of course, many others involved in the productions who work behind the scenes. Some of those—such as Jim Elder, who was a statistical whiz backing up football announcers—also did some broadcasting of their own.

Harry King said that Elder's index card system enabled him to access what a player had done in the past. King said that Elder "could tell the play-by-play announcer what the player had done the last time the player had an opportunity, such as whether the player had kicked the ball 42 yards or returned the ball for 11." Rick Schaeffer has played key roles both behind the microphone and behind the scenes, and Chuck Barrett gained experience as a producer for football broadcasts in addition to doing baseball play-by-play before becoming the football and basketball announcer. James Dokes, who was telecommunications supervisor for KATV, was in the key role of director of field operations and involved in radio and TV game coverage for many years.

Another important "spot" on Razorback football broadcasts is the role of spotter—the individual who helps the play-by-play announcer identify which players are in on the action. For many years that role has been filled by Bob Carver, an automobile dealer from Mena. In 1970, he was watching a Hog football practice with Orville Henry, Bud Campbell, and Coach Broyles. Campbell mentioned that he needed someone to serve as a spotter and Henry said, "Get Bob to do it, he's going to the game anyway." That began a role that was to last more than 40 years.

Carver said that during games he utilizes two boards: one for offense and one for defense. He explained that he works with jersey names and numbers, and since he watches a lot of practice and a lot of film, he is able to help the play-by-play announcer see things the announcer might otherwise have missed. "I don't watch running backs so much," Carver said. "You're going to eventually see who's carrying the ball anyway. I watch the interior linemen, and tell the people in the booth who makes the good blocks that help spring the running back."

He noted that over the years the booth remained small, but the number of people in the booth has increased, and the broadcast has expanded. Carver said that "the other guys in the booth always kid me," about his ability to determine whether a team has achieved a first down. "They ask me how I can tell before the measurement whether the offense has a first down or has come up short. They want to know how I do that. I tell them if I told them how I do it, I'd lose my job, because they would be stealing my stuff."

He named the 1978 Orange Bowl, in which Arkansas upset Oklahoma, as his favorite game, with the 50–48 win over LSU in 2007 also ranking high. Among players, he particularly pointed to Joe Ferguson, Ron Calcagni, Billy Ray Smith Jr., Bill Montgomery, and Chuck Dicus.

From the broadcast crew, he said he was fortunate to work with Bud Campbell, "the unbelievable play-by-play man," and Paul Eells, "who I worked with 28 years, and through those years never had a greater mentor." He said it was tough for all involved with the broadcasts when Eells died, "but now that Chuck Barrett and Keith Jackson are working together, you just can't get any better than that."

Changes in Technology and Broadcasting Rights

Rick Schaeffer has seen many changes in the technology involved in broadcasting. "We used to use a business phone line and carried all of our equipment in two trunks that weighed about 80-something pounds total," he said. "I know because when we played at Vanderbilt the broadcast booth was way up there and there was no elevator, so I was drenched by the time I carried up the equipment. Now, the equipment is lighter and we get a better quality broadcast. We use an ISDN (Integrated Services Digital

Network) line now and the quality is much better than a regular phone line. I'm sure the equipment will continue to get lighter."

Schaeffer challenges himself to be the best he can on the air and to think of the Razorback fans who are listening. "They re-member the things you say, so you have to be careful. You have to remember to be uplifting and encouraging. I realize that for a lot of people in Arkansas, when they tune into the game it is the highlight of their day."

Schaeffer has also seen changes in the administration and management of Razorback broadcasting rights, up through the current agreement with IMG. When Schaeffer first came to UA, the Snider Corporation of Little Rock distributed the broadcasts through the Arkansas Radio Network (ARN). Then, the Southwest Conference wanted the broadcasts back under confer-ence control. He found that arrangement to be "a disaster" when each competing team had a representative in the broadcast booth. "For instance, if a game against Baylor was in Fayetteville, the play-by-play guy would be provided by Arkansas and the color guy would be provided by Baylor." That arrangement didn't last long, and Learfield Sports, which started out with the University of Missouri in 1975, handled the broadcasts for about four years. At that time, Learfield managed broadcasts for a number of college teams, including Alabama, Iowa, and Oklahoma. In 1995, the Arkansas Razorback Sports Network (ARSN), associated with KATV in Little Rock, won the broadcast rights. Since KATV had long enjoyed a close association with the Razorbacks, this was an ideal relationship at the time. That close connection was solidified with Eells, KATV's sports director, serving as the voice of Razorback football and also doing the coach's shows for basketball.

However, following Eells's death and Mike Nail's year as in-terim football play-by-play man, it was time for a new football voice to be chosen. There was considerable speculation and some controversy over who would be the choice to become the football play-by-play announcer in 2007, following Nail's one-year assignment after Eells died.

Mike Nail became a familiar voice of Razorback basketball and was additionally involved in football coverage over the years. He was also a sports anchor for several TV stations in Northwest Arkansas.

Chuck Barrett became a triple threat—announcing Razorback baseball, football, and basketball, and hosting the coaches' shows made it a grand slam.

6. Into a New Millennium: Chuck Barrett, Little Rock, and Fayetteville

UA athletic director Frank Broyles made clear that his choice for football play-by-play announcer was Chuck Barrett, the long-time baseball announcer for the Razorbacks who had also been part of the football broadcast crew for 12 years. However, KATV general manager Dale Nicholson favored Scott Inman, KATV news anchor and longtime host for ARSN's scoreboard show. Inman, who grew up in Stuttgart, Arkansas, had also filled in on some Razorback basketball broadcasts and had considerable sports broadcasting experience at Arkansas State University in Jonesboro.

Indeed, Nicholson and KATV believed they were entitled to designate the football play-by-play announcer. Even though ARSN at the time was a division of KATV, Broyles and the university insisted that it was their choice to make. Some depicted this as a Little Rock vs. Northwest Arkansas conflict, a carry-over from the "stadium debate" of 1999–2000, when there was dispute over how many, if any, Razorback games would be played at Little Rock's War Memorial Stadium. By that time, the Fayetteville stadium was undergoing renovation and additions that would significantly increase its capacity over that of War Memorial, and some believed that all home games should be played on the university campus. However, Little Rock business and political leaders—along with many fans from central, southern, and eastern Arkansas—strongly favored the Razorbacks continuing to play some games in Little Rock. For some of those fans, the Little Rock games were among life's most treasured rituals. The fervor of the debate was indicative of how seriously Arkansas fans take Razorback football.

Broyles favored playing five games annually in Fayetteville, which would help raise funds to finance the stadium expansion on campus. Since War Memorial's opening in 1948, Arkansas had usually split its home games between Little Rock and Fayetteville. From 1944 up until 2000, the Razorbacks normally played only three games per season in Fayetteville and played three or four times per year at Little Rock. When there was an odd number of home games, Little Rock had usually landed the extra one. If five games were played in Fayetteville as Broyles proposed, that would have left War Memorial with only two games and, in some years, just one.

After considerable discussion and some heated debate, an agreement was reached whereby the Razorbacks would play three games in Little Rock in two of the following 15 years and two games the rest of the time. However, in 2008, a new contract was signed between the university and the War Memorial Stadium Commission, which extended the agreement through the 2016 season, with the Razorbacks playing twice annually in Little Rock, including at least one SEC game each year. In return for this two-year extension, the requirement of three Little Rock games in two years of the original agreement was dropped.

Making the announcement of the 2008 agreement, Athletic Director Jeff Long, Frank Broyles's successor, said, "The Razorbacks are important to this entire state, and we know playing in Little Rock and central Arkansas is important to the entire state." He noted that there was none of the acrimony that surrounded the 2000 stadium controversy.

The competition between Chuck Barrett and Scott Inman was not really a replay of the stadium debate either, even though some saw it that way. Despite Inman's on-air ability and his KATV connection, Barrett seemed like a natural and popular choice for the football play-by-play position. As UA baseball had received growing attention, Barrett had become increasingly well known around the state as the voice of Razorback baseball since 1992. He also had been part of the broadcast team for football as executive producer of the broadcasts for 11 years and he had served as ARSN pre-game and halftime show host. Barrett was also familiar to many sports fans because of the call-in radio show that he hosted, *Sports Rap*. The popular show began in Fayetteville and eventually could be heard throughout most of Arkansas. He gave up that program, which had a 13-year run, when he took the football play-by-play role, which also involved his becoming a member of the athletic department staff at Arkansas.

In May 2007, Nicholson wrote a letter to Broyles asserting that KATV was entitled to the "final decision" in designating the broadcaster. "Coach, while we are hopeful we can reach an accord on this announcement, KATV feels strongly that having a play-by-play announcer who is also connected with KATV is vitally important." (*Arkansas Business* newspaper obtained the correspondence through a Freedom of Information request.) In a later letter, Nicholson said that he was "sorry we don't see eye-to-eye on the play-by-play announcer for the University of Arkansas football radio broadcasts, and frankly, was quite surprised since you expressed no objection when we presented the idea of Scott

Inman filling this role more than six months ago to you in your office and you have articulated none until your letter...in which you stated that your choice is Chuck Barrett."

Broyles then replied by stating that he did not view the choice of Inman as being in the best interest of the university or Razorback football. "I am very disappointed and surprised that KATV would now assert, for the first time, that it has the 'right' to select and to publicize a new play-by-play announcer in disregard of the University's right of approval and its best interests." Indeed, Broyles said he believed that a unilateral selection and announcement of Inman "would be a breach of contract and a breach of the fiduciary duties owed to the University under the license agreement."

Broyles also said that KNWA, the NBC television affiliate in Fayetteville that was then carrying the football coach's TV show, said it would not carry the weekly coach's show if Inman, the news anchor for KATV in Little Rock, was selected. Broyles pointed out that the play-by-play announcer had traditionally been the host for the coach's show and if the show was not carried in Northwest Arkansas, it would create a financial hardship for the university.

"The University of Arkansas appreciates the long-time, mutually beneficial relationship we have enjoyed with KATV," Broyles wrote to Nicholson, "but we must make the best decision for our football program." He added, "While KATV is the current operator of the network, ultimately it is the University's network, which is why we hold the final approval of any talent."

As columnist David McCollum of the Conway newspaper the *Log Cabin Democrat* noted, more and more play-by-play announcers were working directly for a university as opposed to the previous practice of having a journalist connected to a television station, often as a sports anchor, do the broadcasts.

Chuck Barrett's Expanded Role

Although Chuck Barrett took on the football play-by-play responsibilities, Scott Inman continued working on game broadcasts as the pre-game show and post-game *Scoreboard Show*
co-host along with former Hog football great Quinn Grovey.
Inman also was the announcer for early-season TV broadcasts of
the basketball Razorbacks.

Clay Henry, publisher of *Hawgs Illustrated*, the magazine for
Razorback fans, said when Barrett got the football play-by-play job
that Chuck was someone who had paid his dues. He compared
Barrett in this respect to Campbell, Eells, and sports journalists
such as Harry King, Jim Elder, and Clay's father, Orville Henry, all
of whom were longtime fixtures in covering the Razorbacks. Clay
Henry said that what Barrett "brings to the table is just what he
gives to a Razorback baseball play-by-play broadcast." Henry said
of Barrett, "He has the right amount of excitement in his voice,
just enough to where you can still know what is happening as you
raise your fist to punctuate a big play with him."

There was plenty of excitement in Barrett's voice when he
made what is probably the most famous and widely recognized
baseball call:

> That ball is gone! That's a grand slam home run! Brady Toops just hit a
> grand slam home run.

That memorable call came when catcher Brady Toops hit a
ninth-inning grand slam on June 6, 2004, in the NCAA regional
at Baum Stadium. The home run led to an 11–9 Arkansas come-
from-behind victory over Wichita State in what was an elimination game for the Hogs. It was a key step in the team's march to
the 2004 College World Series. In 2011, it was selected as the

most memorable moment in the first 15 years of Baum Stadium, and the highlight video with Barrett's excited exclamation was frequently replayed on the stadium scoreboard's video screen.

Another classic call from Barrett came in the 2009 College World Series when Arkansas faced Virginia in an elimination game and the Hogs were down to their last out:

> They are not holding Cox on...here's the one-one...swung on...skyed in to left—that ball is hit pretty well—It is gone! Brett Eibner has hit a home run and the ball game is tied! Brett Eibner has hit a home run and the ball game is tied! The Razorbacks down to their final out ...and Eibner has just saved things. A two-run homer to left field and we have a 3–3 ball game... Wow! What a moment.

Arkansas won the game 4–3 in the tenth inning and finished tied for third in the CWS that year.

Many Razorback fans remember the improbable victory over Baylor in the 2012 baseball super-regional in Waco with the Hogs on the verge of elimination. Two successive Arkansas batters were hit by pitches with the bases loaded in the bottom of the ninth, giving the Hogs a 5–4 win. Here's the way Barrett described the bizarre ending of the game:

> Reeves stands in and waits and the left-hander comes set and delivers. The pitch is inside—He Hit Him!...And Arkansas wins. We're coming back tomorrow. They hit two batters with the bases loaded and we're coming back tomorrow. The Hogs win it 5–4.

And that next day's game proved to be another thriller, a tenth-inning 1–0 victory that sent Arkansas to the College World Series in Omaha. This was Barrett's excited description as Baylor's Dan Evatt batted, with Colby Suggs on the mound for Arkansas:

> Two balls, two strikes. Suggs delivers. Swing and a MISS! He Struck Him Out!—The Hogs are going to Omaha. The Razorbacks have beaten Baylor and we have a mob scene on the field.

"When you turn on the radio and hear his voice, you know it's the Razorbacks," Rick Schaeffer told Rich Polikoff of the *Arkansas Democrat-Gazette.* "Everybody liked Chuck, but where his career got a lift was that grand slam by Brady Toops. That's his signature call and just stamped him as the voice of the Razorbacks."

Barrett told Chris Bahn of ArkansasSports360.com that announcing a baseball game is like writing a novel. Brevity of words can be used in both, but the more detail, the better it is when it comes to storytelling and baseball announcing. Barrett is effective at painting a picture of what is occurring in the ballpark or stadium. That is characteristic of some of the great sports announcers such as Vin Scully, the longtime voice of the Los Angeles Dodgers.

"If you really got down to brass tacks you could tell the story in 75 pages instead of 300. It wouldn't be any good. You wouldn't set it up. You wouldn't paint the picture. You wouldn't do all the things necessary to tell the story well. Baseball gives you the time to do that." Barrett said he wished there was more downtime in football. "That downtime is what gives you the opportunity to really connect with the listener." Most fans, however, would say that Barrett does connect with the listeners, whatever the sport.

Becoming the lead announcer for Razorback sports is a dream for many in Arkansas. "When you're a broadcaster and you have grown up in Arkansas, you obviously dream of this," Barrett said. "There is an awesome sense of responsibility to the Razorback fans to do a good job. To give the information they want to hear in the appropriate amount of time is the key." Like Mike Nail, Barrett says that he was one of those who would listen to games in his room. "I would shut the door so no one would come in and would keep stats on a notebook. There are listeners who do that as well, so I always need to be clear and accurate."

As Barrett was growing up, Jack Buck, the legendary St. Louis Cardinals baseball broadcaster, was his favorite big-time broadcaster. "Listening to Jack Buck is how I fell in love with sports in the late '60s and early '70s." He noted that there were only three channels then and no ESPN. "There was the Game of the Week on Saturday and later some Monday night baseball. My parents got me a small radio. I listened to baseball games in my bed at night," Barrett recalled, adding that Buck's voice was often the last one he heard before going to sleep. He points out that Buck broadcast both baseball and football for many years. Indeed, among Buck's football assignments was TV play-by-play of the 1965 Arkansas-LSU Cotton Bowl game. And, interestingly, many of the radio stations that carried Razorback broadcasts, particularly in the early years, also carried the Cardinals games during the major league baseball season, and the Cardinals have long had a devoted following in Arkansas. Stations such as KFFA in Helena and KAGH in Crossett have long carried both the Cardinals and the Razorbacks. In 2012, 18 Arkansas radio stations were part of the Cardinals network, and many of them also were part of the Razorback network.

Rick Schaeffer, who works with Barrett on Razorback baseball broadcasts (as well as basketball), noted that when they were growing up, both he and Barrett wanted to be major league baseball announcers but are "very happy and very lucky" to be doing Razorback baseball and connected with a great college program. Many listeners believe the two are major-league caliber.

"I am probably the luckiest guy around," Barrett said after being named to the football play-by-play position in addition to his baseball role. He recalled that his mother made sure that he and his sister could see a Razorback game in Fayetteville every year when they were growing up. He remembers sitting in what were then the south end-zone bleachers and thinking about one day being able to buy a ticket to sit along the sideline. "Every once in a while, when I am in the booth, I can see that scene in my mind's eye."

"I'm a lucky guy and I have never taken that for granted," Barrett said. "It is a unique privilege to do what I do. There are a lot of people out there who could do just as good of a job. But, for whatever reason, they have not been in the right place at the right time. I've just been lucky and it is a privilege to have this job."

Barrett said that in taking over the football announcing, it was a little overwhelming, following the legendary Paul Eells, and said that he would tell the story his own way and not try to mimic others. Not surprisingly, however, some do hear traces of Eells's influence in Barrett's broadcasts. "I don't think anyone should try to be Paul Eells, just like Paul didn't try to be like Bud Campbell," Barrett said. "I understand that to sports fans in this state, the Razorbacks are an important part of their lives. That is what I think is so special about being the play-by-play man for any team. You become the fan's companion. Paul made people feel like they were at the stadium."

"The thing that made Paul so special to so many fans is that he talked to them and not at them," Barrett said. "There are a lot of people under 50 who take for granted that everyone has cable. Not everyone does. There are people who live in rural areas of the state who can't see or the older ones who are part of the radio generation who rely on the play-by-play man to vocally take them to the game."

"I watched Paul when I was growing up," Barrett added, noting that he was just glad to be part of the football crew with Eells. "As we went along, I found out what a great person and team player Paul was. If he would have played, he would have been a great team player. He never thought he was more important than anybody on the crew, whether the person was holding a camera or carrying cables."

Chuck Barrett was born in Memphis but grew up in Clarksville, Arkansas. He recalls attending his first Razorback football game in 1972 when he was nine. Only a few years later, at age 16, he got his start as a play-by-play announcer, serving as the public address announcer for youth league baseball games in Clarksville. His first football play-by-play work came in 1981. "Somehow, I got the chance to do play-by-play for the football games at Clarksville," Barrett told Quinton Bagley of the *Russellville Courier*. He did the Clarksville Panthers high school games for several years and also worked for KARV, a Russellville radio station, and handled a number of sports assignments in addition to other duties.

He then moved on to Fort Smith, where he did football play-by-play broadcasts for area high school games. Barrett served as news director for KMAG radio in Fort Smith, but he wanted to concentrate on sports and wasn't sure that was going to work out. However, he got an opportunity and what turned out to be a big break when he heard that the Razorback baseball broadcasting job might be open. Scott Miller, who had been doing the broadcasts, was leaving. He had succeeded Glen Adams, who had been the first to broadcast Razorback baseball. Mike Nail and writer Nate Allen had also done a few games.

Barrett quickly applied for a job at KFAY radio in Fayetteville, which carried the UA baseball broadcasts at the time. Before applying for the job, he didn't have any tapes of himself doing play-by-play so he went outside where he could find some background noise, imagined a game taking place, and called the action as he saw it in his head. He got the job with KFAY as news director and doing Razorback baseball. "I had an opportunity at a very young age to do something that I wanted to do, so I took advantage of it," Barrett said. "Now, I can't imagine ever doing anything else."

He credited KFAY and Demaree Media, which owned the station, with helping him get his foot in the door. Barrett began doing Razorback baseball in 1992, the year Arkansas began competing in the SEC. Within a couple of years, he took over the *Sports Rap* call-in radio show that had been started by Mike Nail and became part of the Razorback football broadcasting team. He began by working in the studio doing a halftime and scoreboard show from KARN radio in Little Rock. In 1995, he joined former Razorback football great Joe Ferguson in hosting a pre-game show for ARSN. Two years later, Ferguson became part of Danny Ford's coaching staff, and that's when another former Hog quarterback, Quinn Grovey, joined the broadcast team as part of the pre-game show and as the sideline announcer.

Baseball announcing can be a grind, with games sometimes continuing for three or four hours and games often scheduled on several consecutive days. And college baseball involves long road trips, frequently by bus. Regardless, Barrett has a talent for keeping things interesting in his broadcasts, displaying a keen knowledge of the game, and keeping listeners well informed about what is happening.

"Not only is he talented as a play-by-play man, he's helped the UA to do something that few thought was possible just a few years ago—take a baseball network statewide in a big way," wrote Clay Henry of *Hawgs Illustrated*. "Chuck did that by riding the bus with the team for all of those games. How would you like to finish a broadcast at 3 p.m. Sunday in Auburn, Alabama, then get on a bus for a 15-hour trip home just in time to do your morning broadcasts?" Barrett was also doing morning sports reports for several Arkansas radio stations.

Barrett is joined in the broadcast booth by Rick Schaeffer for home baseball games and some post-season contests, including the 2012 College World Series in Omaha. Schaeffer provides commentary and analysis and handles an inning or so of play-by-play. Schaeffer's extensive knowledge of Arkansas sports history adds to the strength of the baseball broadcasts.

Not surprisingly, Barrett developed a close relationship with the Razorback baseball coaches. Norm DeBriyn, who coached through the 2002 season, was the first coach Barrett had significant interaction with. It was DeBriyn who built Razorback baseball into a nationally respected program. "Norm's a great man, a unique individual. He was the first major coach I had worked with on the major college level. Working with him was the first time I understood the obsession with winning coaches on this level have. It is a mental grind on these guys."

Barrett has done literally hundreds of interviews with DeBriyn's successor, Dave Van Horn, who played under DeBriyn and became the Arkansas baseball coach in 2003. Barrett said one of Van Horn's best qualities is that he can say so much in a short broadcast slot. "He can say more in four minutes than just about anybody I know. You ask a direct question, you get a direct answer. You know, football coaches have that military or bunker mentality. You have to speak in 'coach speak' with them. You have to be careful not to let anyone know what they will be doing on Saturday. You can't give away the game plan. Coach Van Horn and baseball coaches in general, by contrast, are very direct in what they say during an interview."

Barrett said, "The biggest thing about interviewing coaches is that when you have a question, there is a time and place to ask. You get to know this very quickly." Barrett remembers a difficult Thanksgiving Day with former Arkansas football coach Danny

Ford. "You know, I liked Danny Ford an awful lot. And man, 1997 was a tough year." By late in the season, it had become apparent that Ford would not be returning as the Razorbacks coach. "When we played in Baton Rouge in 1997, everyone knew that he would be fired over the weekend. It was Thanksgiving, so we all got together for a meal, and Coach Ford said the Thanksgiving blessing. Everybody put on a brave front, but it was sad."

Ford was succeeded by Houston Nutt, and his first year was a dramatic success. Interest in Razorback football sky-rocketed. The 1998 team reeled off eight straight victories before a crushing last-minute loss to number-one Tennessee. An indication of the high level of interest generated in 1998 was seen in the size of the audience for the Houston Nutt television show. Hosted by Paul Eells and carried by KATV, the show drew exceptional audience ratings as the season progressed, averaging a 33 share in Central Arkansas in the November 1998 ratings period, despite airing at 10:30 p.m. on Sundays. That means that 33 percent of the TVs actually in use at the time in the area were tuned in to watch Nutt's game reviews and pep talks. "I just wish he was available to anchor," KATV news director Bob Steel said at the time, a time when Nutt's popularity was at a peak. The *Arkansas Times*, a Little Rock–based weekly newspaper, named Nutt as Arkansan of the Year. Nutt was hailed by no less than Orville Henry, the longtime chronicler of the Razorbacks, as the answer to fans' prayers.

Although there were significant high points during the Nutt era, the final years of his tenure were marked by divisiveness in the Razorback Nation. A noisy faction was clamoring for Nutt to be replaced, which occurred at the end of the 2007 season, with Nutt taking a large buy-out package and heading to Ole Miss, where he was the head coach from 2008 to 2011. Some of the anti-Nutt faction associated Barrett with Nutt, and there was some minor grumbling on message boards and the Internet about Barrett being named to the football play-by-play slot. This may have owed in part to an infamous incident that incited Nutt's critics.

After a 28–15 victory over Ole Miss at Oxford in November 2005, in what was an overall disappointing season for Arkansas, Nutt, in his regular post-game locker-room radio interview, was asked by Barrett about a game-turning touchdown pass by Casey Dick. "I called that play, Chuck," an exuberant Nutt exclaimed. Nutt's critics took this as an unsubtle rejoinder to complaints that he should turn over the offensive coordinator/play-calling role to someone else. Because that quote was cited so often by Nutt's detractors, some associated Barrett with it. Some of those same critics suggested Barrett was a "homer," with only good things to say about the Razorbacks on his call-in radio show.

Home-Team Favorites

"Certainly they don't expect the Razorback play-by-play man to be any less of a home team rah-rah guy, do they?" asked sports columnist Jim Harris of SportingLifeArkansas.com. Traditionally, play-by-play announcers for a specific team—college or professional—see things from the perspective of that team and its fans and certainly that was true of the best-known of the Arkansas broadcasters: Cheyne, Campbell, Eells, Nail, et al.

Gravel-voiced Larry Munson, the longtime University of Georgia announcer, avoided any pretense of objectivity when he was broadcasting Bulldogs' games. He was an unapologetic Georgia fan. "I've never known a play-by-play man for a university or a team who is not unapologetically biased and shows an overflowing enthusiasm for the team he serves," said *Log Cabin Democrat* sports columnist David McCollum.

Blake Eddins, who did color commentary for some of the TV coverage of Razorback basketball after his playing days, said in 2011, "I get in trouble for saying 'we' too much, but this is the Arkansas Razorback Sports Network after all."

Unlike announcers for national networks such as ESPN, every radio and television broadcaster for the 30 major league baseball teams is either paid by the team or is hired with that team's approval, and they usually make it clear that they are pulling for the team that directly or indirectly employs them. Harry Caray and Jack Buck, for example, who are often cited as an influence on Arkansas broadcasters, left no doubt that they were pulling for the Cardinals, and, in Caray's case, later he was backing the Chicago Cubs when he became that team's regular announcer.

Although Barrett, like other voices of the Razorbacks, leaves no doubt that he backs the Razorbacks, he—as have the other voices—tries to tell it like it is, even when things go badly for the Hogs. In a 2011 NCAA regional baseball game, for example, Barrett described this setback for Arkansas: "He [the first-baseman] just dropped it. It should have been a routine play. It's an error on the first baseman. The Hogs should be out of the inning."

To the surprise of no one who was familiar with Barrett's work on baseball broadcasts, he quickly seemed comfortably at home in handling football play-by-play. While most Razorback fans think highly of the broadcasters, as with other aspects of Razorback sports, they sometimes debate the merits of announcers and offer critiques on message boards and social media.

Although he maintained the "Touchdown Arkansas" trademark from the Eells years, which had become a tradition with Arkansas fans, in short order Barrett proved that the qualities that served him well in baseball broadcasts also carried over to football. He can be calm and methodical, but—without getting too carried away—he leaves little doubt when something exciting is happening on the field.

Although 2008 was not a great season for Arkansas football, Barrett was behind the mike for a spectacular Razorback victory over LSU in Little Rock in what was dubbed the "Miracle on Markham II."

This is how Barrett called the score that gave Arkansas a 31–30 come-from-behind win over the Tigers with 26 seconds remaining in the game:

> *Casey Dick in the shotgun, gets the snap, wants to throw—deep down the right side for Crawford…Touchdown Arkansas!*

Anyone listening closely could hear analyst Keith Jackson's excited "Ha! Ha!" in the background.

Two years later, the 31–23 Arkansas victory over LSU before a packed stadium in Little Rock and a CBS national TV audience in November 2010 pushed the Razorbacks into a BCS Sugar Bowl slot. It was memorable for a number of big plays.

The excitement was apparent in Barrett's calls of some of the major scoring plays for Arkansas that day:

> *Touchdown Arkansas! Knile Davis goes 13 yards, and the Razorbacks are on the board!*

> *Hamilton's gonna go. Touchdown Arkansas! Cobi Hamilton, 85 yards, and just like that the Hogs strike!*

> *Fifteen seconds left in the half…Mallet's gonna throw—complete to Cobi Hamilton at mid-field. Cobi breaks a tackle. He's at the 40, the 30, the 20. Touchdown Arkansas! Eighty yards. On the last play of the half.*

On the radio coverage of that second Ryan Mallet–to–Cobi Hamilton touchdown pass, a second voice could also be heard: *Wow!* That was the comment of color analyst Keith Jackson.

Other Razorback Voices

Keith Jackson had become a familiar voice to Razorback fans. Although a Little Rock native, he played college football at the University of Oklahoma from 1984 to 1987 and was a standout tight end on the national championship team at OU in 1985 and an All-American in 1986 and 1987. He followed that with a highly successful pro career with the Philadelphia Eagles, Miami Dolphins, and Green Bay Packers, and was a six-time Pro Bowl selection and three-time All-Pro. He began working as a color commentator and analyst for the Razorback football radio broadcasts in 2000. His son, Keith Jackson Jr., played defensive line for Arkansas from 2003 to 2006.

Jackson is not to be confused with the famed ABC sportscaster of the same name, with whom Frank Broyles worked on ABC college football telecasts, 1977–1985. ABC's Jackson— who was famous for such phrases as "Whoa, Nellie!"—made a surprise visit to take part in the ceremonies honoring Broyles at the South Carolina game in Fayetteville in November 2007 when Frank Broyles Field at Reynolds Razorback Stadium was dedicated. It was a special night for Razorback fans, with the Hogs rolling over South Carolina 48–36 behind a 321-yard rushing performance by Darren McFadden.

While Broyles provided color commentary and analysis for ABC's Jackson, Arkansas's Keith Jackson plays that role for Barrett as he did earlier for Eells and Nail. Razorback fans came to appreciate Jackson's insight and inside football knowledge and experience. Barrett and Jackson got to know each other during the years that Barrett was part of the football broadcast crew and worked together easily when Barrett took on the play-by-play role.

Returning to his home state of Arkansas after being an All-American at Oklahoma and starring in the NFL, Keith Jackson became a popular and respected color commentator and analyst for Razorback football broadcasts beginning in 2000.

Before taking on the football play-by-play responsibilities, Barrett had worked on pre-game broadcasts with Joe Ferguson and Quinn Grovey, two of the greatest Arkansas quarterbacks. Both were named to the Razorback All-Century team. Ferguson played from 1970 to 1972 and Grovey 1987 to 1990.

"When I was a kid, Joe Ferguson was the man," Barrett said. "My mother let me stay up late to watch Joe play quarterback with Buffalo as a rookie. I remember seeing Joe play [as a Razorback] against Texas in the rain in Little Rock in 1971, so to work with Joe on the pre-game broadcast was an overwhelming treat." When he began working with Ferguson on Razorback broadcasts in 1995, Barrett said, "I remember looking over many times saying to myself, 'Wow, man, this is Joe Ferguson.'"

After Ferguson joined Danny Ford's coaching staff, Grovey became a fixture on the broadcast team, working on pre-game shows and handling sideline analysis during games. "I admired Quinn as a player," Barrett said, "and I've enjoyed working with him on the broadcast. He's a terrific guy." Arkansas fans are accustomed to hearing Barrett say, "Let's go down to Quinn," for Grovey's sideline analysis and reports.

Barrett added to his football and baseball radio responsibilities by taking on the basketball job after Nail retired, becoming the lead announcer for all three major sports. Rick Schaeffer, who had worked with Nail for many years, continued as the basketball color commentator and statistical maestro, having already teamed up with Barrett on the baseball broadcasts. Schaeffer had been part of the basketball broadcast team for 23 years up until 2000 before resuming that position in the 2004–2005 season.

Former Razorback basketball star Joe Kleine handled the role of analyst on the radio broadcasts for four years, 2000–2004. After starring for the Razorbacks from 1983 to 1985, Kleine had a lengthy professional career, with 15 years in the NBA, and was a member of the Chicago Bulls championship team in 1998. He was also a member of the U.S. gold-medal basketball team in the 1984 Olympics.

Several former Razorback athletes have moved successfully into broadcasting following their playing days. Probably the best known as a broadcaster was Pat Summerall, who played football for Arkansas 1949–1951 as an end and place-kicker. He then played ten years in the NFL, most notably for the New York Giants, and began his broadcast career covering the Giants; in the years that followed, he became a broadcasting giant. He started working on NFL telecasts on CBS in 1964, first as a color commentator and then as play-by-play man, a role he continued for CBS and Fox for most of the next 40 years. For 22 of those years, he partnered with John Madden as the foremost pro football broadcast team. When Summerall died in 2013, Madden said of his longtime broadcast partner, "Pat is the voice of football and always will be." In addition to calling 13 Super Bowls, Summerall was also involved in coverage of 26 Masters golf tournaments and 21 U.S. Opens in tennis. After retiring from regular coverage, Summerall did special assignments, including TV play-by-play of the Cotton Bowl appearance by Arkansas on January 1, 2008. He is a member of the Arkansas Sports Hall of Fame and the University of Arkansas Sports Hall of Fame.

Another with a long stint in radio and TV coverage of the NFL is Dan Hampton, an Arkansas All-American as a defensive tackle in 1978. He was a first-round draft choice of the Chicago Bears and was selected to the Pro Football Hall of Fame after an illustrious career with the Bears. Subsequently, he did color commentary for NBC coverage of the NFL and was co-host for the syndicated *Pro Football Weekly* television show for many years. He also did pre- and post-game shows for Bears games on Chicago radio stations.

Former Razorbacks Jimmy Johnson and Barry Switzer, both of whom went on to successful careers as college and NFL coaches, have also done commentary and analysis for national TV networks. Within Arkansas, former Razorback stars Bruce James, an All-American defensive end in 1970, and David Bazzel, a Hog linebacker 1981–1985, have appeared on local TV shows analyzing Razorback football. Marcus Elliot, an offensive guard, 1982–1984, has been a regular on radio's statewide *Drive Time Sports*, and basketball sharp-shooter Pat Bradley, 1996–1999, became a Little Rock sports radio personality. Matt Jones, former Razorback quarterback, also became a co-host for a radio show, as sports talk radio boomed in Arkansas in the second decade of the twenty-first century, with much of the programming related to discussion of Razorback sports

Scott Hastings was a Razorback basketball standout from 1979 to 1982 and played 11 seasons in the NBA, including a stint with the Denver Nuggets. He then became a well-known voice in the Denver area with a sports-talk show and as an analyst on Nuggets' broadcasts.

Jimmy Dykes, another former Razorback basketball player, has been a longtime analyst for some of the games televised by the Arkansas network, originally working with Paul Eells, beginning in 1994. Normally, these are early-season games played before the conference schedule begins. Eells did the play-by-play for most of these TV games for 29 years until his death in 2006. He was succeeded in that role by Scott Inman, his KATV colleague.

Inman and Dykes teamed up on the pay-per-view telecast of the 2011 Arkansas football opener with Missouri State. Inman handled the play-by-play and Dykes provided color commentary. Basketball coach Mike Anderson served as a special guest commentator and said excitedly, "Watch out, this could be one," as punt returner Joe Adams began one of his two sensational touchdown runs in the game.

Dykes, a 1985 UA graduate, originally wanted to be a basketball coach and got some good experience working as an assistant to Eddie Sutton, including stints at Kentucky and Oklahoma State. However, it was in broadcasting that Dykes became nationally known and respected. In addition to his work on Razorback games, Dykes began to get some limited assignments as an analyst on ESPN basketball coverage in 1995–1996 and eventually became a regular featured analyst on ESPN, covering dozens of major college games each season.

He has often teamed with play-by-play announcer Brad Nessler on SEC basketball games on ESPN, including a number of Arkansas games.

Others who served as analysts for the televised basketball games on the Arkansas network included Ray Tucker, Little Rock sportscaster, and Bill Rogers, who was an assistant sports information director at Arkansas. In more recent years, Blake Eddins, a former Razorback player under Nolan Richardson and Stan Heath, has been an analyst for the TV games on the Arkansas network, working with Scott Inman.

Although televised UA basketball games were once a rarity, it is now rare for a game not to be televised. The 2004–2005 media guide noted that 85 Razorback games had been televised over the past four years. By contrast, as late as the 1970s and early 1980s, only a limited number of games were televised, and some of those were available only on a late-night tape-delayed basis. However, by the 2009–2010 season, 25 games were on the TV schedule, including six non-conference games on the Razorback Sports Network consisting of stations in Fayetteville-Fort Smith, Little Rock, and Jonesboro. Other appearances were on the ESPN family of networks, Fox Sports Net, Comcast Sports Southeast, and the SEC Network. The SEC Tournament was also televised.

Chuck Barrett: A Triple Threat

It was widely expected that when Mike Nail retired from the basketball play-by-play role, Chuck Barrett would succeed him, becoming the voice of the Razorbacks for the three major men's sports. And, indeed, Barrett took on the basketball assignment with the beginning of the 2010–2011 season, becoming a year-round, full-time voice of the Razorbacks.

"For nearly 20 years, fans throughout Arkansas have listened to Chuck Barrett describe some of the most memorable moments in Razorback history," Athletic Director Jeff Long said. "When fans tune in and hear Chuck's distinctive delivery, they immediately know they are following the Hogs and are undoubtedly listening to the voice of the Razorbacks. For 29 seasons, Mike Nail brought Arkansas basketball into the homes of Razorback fans. I have no doubt Chuck will carry on that tradition of excellence in broadcasting Razorback basketball."

Barrett said he was "humbled to follow one of Arkansas's legendary broadcasters in this position," and noted that "for decades, radio broadcasts have helped bring our entire state together behind the Razorbacks." He said he was appreciative of the opportunity "to be a small part of the special relationship between our state and the Razorbacks."

It is important to understand the true passion of Razorback fans, Barrett said. "Every fan I've had an encounter with, I identify with, because it wasn't very long ago that that's what I was," Barrett told the *Democrat-Gazette*'s Rich Polikoff for a featured profile in the newspaper.

With his broader broadcasting responsibilities, Barrett encountered some overlap in football, basketball, and baseball seasons. For example, in 2011, basketball and baseball schedules intersected and made it impossible for him to do play-by-play for all the games in both sports. Early in the baseball season, Phil Elson broadcast a series of Razorback games at San Diego State, which conflicted with the SEC basketball tournament, and Kyle Kellams, news director for KUAF, the university's public radio station, did the play-by-play for two Saturday games that conflicted with the basketball schedule. Elson was the regular broadcaster for the Arkansas Travelers

Class AA team in the Texas League and has covered other sports in central Arkansas.

In 2012, Kellams broadcast the Houston College Classic games from Minute Maid Park when the Razorback baseball team matched up against Texas Tech, Houston, and Texas in a series of games, which came on the same weekend as a basketball game at Mississippi State. In addition to filling in for Barrett on baseball games, Kellams had also broadcast Razorback women's basketball and soccer. Kevin Trainor, sports information director and later associate athletic director for public relations, also helped out with some baseball broadcasts in earlier years.

Inman and Eddins provided the radio coverage of the Arkansas basketball team's participation in the Las Vegas Invitational basketball tournament in November 2012, as Barrett was in Fayetteville for the Arkansas-LSU football game.

Barrett says he has many great memories of covering Razorback sports, but he particularly remembers his first football game as play-by-play man—"and it had nothing to do with the outcome of the game." As he told John Justus of *Inside Razorback Athletics*, "I had done baseball for so many years that handling the broadcast had become almost instinctive, I knew football would be different and I worked really hard to be prepared and thought I was ready, but once that game began, I realize that I still had lots to learn."

For Razorback fans listening to Barrett, it was certainly not apparent that he was anything other than comfortable in the play-by-play role and in command of the broadcasts. And when he took on basketball broadcasting, he quickly seemed a natural fit for the job. Although he appeared to move seamlessly from broadcasting one sport to another, there were occasions when he seemed to be applying terminology from one sport to another. For example, Barrett would often say, "They are going to go get him." By this he meant that the coach was going to the mound to replace the pitcher, bringing in a reliever. Sometimes he would use the same terminology in a basketball broadcast when a player in foul trouble was about to be replaced, even though the scenario is a bit different, because the coach is not actually going on the court to bring in a replacement. But listeners had little doubt what was going on from Barrett's description.

Besides his game-day responsibilities, Barrett has also served as host for the football coach's show televised weekly during the season. Beginning in the summer of 2011, the UA athletic department and RazorVision took over production of the coaches' shows. The Kimpel Hall TV studio in UA's Lemke Department of Journalism was renovated and became the location for the programs, which remained under the IMG umbrella. Journalism students get instruction and hands-on experience in helping produce coverage of UA men's and women's sports events as part of the RazorVision Academy.

Additionally, beginning in 2009, there were weekly radio shows featuring the Razorback football coach. The *Bobby Petrino Live* show was broadcast on radio each Wednesday night during football season from the Catfish Hole restaurant in Fayetteville and carried by 53 stations. Barrett joined the coach on the weekly show, which was broadcast before an audience at the restaurant with questions from the audience and others sent in on the Internet. After Petrino was fired in the spring of 2012, his replacement, John L. Smith, continued with *Razorback Football Live with John L. Smith*, carried by radio stations across the state. Barrett hosted the show, which also featured Razorback players as guests each week.

When Bret Bielema was hired as the UA football coach in late 2012, the announcement and press conference were carried live by several TV and radio stations. The first edition of *The Bret Bielema Show*, a one-hour special hosted by Chuck Barrett, aired in spring 2013. The show focused on the new Razorback coaching staff and previewed the Red-White spring game. Twelve weekly Bielema shows, with Barrett as host, were scheduled during the 2013 football season.

Basketball coaches have also been featured on similar programs. Barrett had also served as host for *John Pelphrey Live*, featuring the basketball coach, with a format similar to the football coach's live show. The radio program was broadcast on Monday nights from Louie's Bar and Grill in Fayetteville during the 2009–10 and 2010–11 seasons.

In 2011, Pelphrey was succeeded by Mike Anderson. The official introduction of Anderson as the new basketball coach was carried live on several Arkansas television stations, and Barrett served as master of ceremonies for an event that drew a sizable crowd, estimated at 5,000, to Bud Walton Arena. Anderson had earlier been an assistant to Nolan Richardson for 17 years at Arkansas, including the national championship year in 1994.

When the 2011–12 basketball season started, Mike Anderson began a weekly radio show on Monday nights, *Mike'd Up*, hosted by Barrett at Louie's and carried by 40 stations from Jonesboro to Texarkana on the Razorback Sports Network. The following year, the show's location was moved to Sassy's Red House restaurant in Fayetteville. Anderson answered questions from those in the audience and from callers. Also, Anderson's TV show, the aptly named *Full-Court Press*, was seen on the Razorback Sports Network television affiliates and also carried on Fox Sports Southwest and Cox Sports on cable/satellite television.

In 2012, *Razorback Baseball with Dave Van Horn* debuted on Cox Sports Television (CST). The 30-minute show featuring the

Razorback coach was seen on the regional network and was available on ArkansasRazorbacks.com. Barrett hosted the show, which included highlights of the previous week's games, an analytical breakdown segment with Coach Van Horn, features on the Razorback baseball program, the baseball program's history and tradition, Razorback student-athletes, and exclusive behind-the-scenes footage of the team such as a feature on what it's like to be on the road with the Razorbacks.

The Sunday Shows

Late Sunday afternoons had been prime time for the football coach's televised show during the heyday of Frank Broyles. However, fall Sunday afternoons increasingly became dominated by televised professional football games, and the Razorback coach's show moved to other times.

By 1982, *The Lou Holtz Show*, exclusively on KATV and hosted by Paul Eells, was seen on Thursday nights at 10:30, live from Fayetteville. Years later, following his long coaching career—with stops at Minnesota, Notre Dame, and South Carolina after Arkansas—Holtz became a TV personality on ESPN college football coverage.

Eventually, later on Sunday evening became the normal time for the televised Arkansas coach's show as well as other weekly wrap-up shows featuring the Razorbacks, usually following the local news programs.

In 2009, for example, *Inside Razorback Football with Bobby Petrino*, hosted by Barrett, aired statewide on Sundays, with the show seen at 10:30 p.m. on KATV in Little Rock, and at 11 p.m. on KNWA and 9 p.m. on KFTA in Northwest Arkansas. It was also seen at various times on Cox Sports Television, Comcast Sports

Southeast, and Fox Sports South and Southwest. And it was also available through RazorVision and at ArkansasRazorbacks.com.

Pat Summerall (second player from left) starred for the Razorbacks and in the NFL, then became the most recognized voice of pro football telecasts. Here he accepts a trophy after kicking the game-winning field goal when Arkansas defeated Texas 16–14 in 1951, the first win over Texas since 1938. Receiving the trophy with Summerall was Dave "Hawg" Hanner, who later starred as a defensive lineman for the Green Bay Packers, and was a Packers' assistant coach for 16 years.

7. Today's Razorback Broadcasting: A Booming Business

Over the years, as technology developed, college sports became more of a big business. Eventually, as a member of the Southeastern Conference, the University of Arkansas would benefit from the SEC's 15-year contract with CBS Sports for televised football and basketball beginning in 2009 and a long-term multi-sport SEC agreement with the ESPN networks. The original deal with ESPN was good for $2.25 billion over 15 years and brought unprecedented benefits for Arkansas. It was supplemented by the 2013 agreement with ESPN to establish the SEC Network.

Contracts with CBS, ESPN, ISP, and IMG

In 2008, the University of Arkansas had agreed to a ten-year deal with ISP Sports, which partnered with a number of major college athletic programs. The agreement guaranteed $73 million during the duration of the ten-year contract. ISP and the University of Arkansas formed Razorback Sports Properties, which is responsible for multimedia rights, including radio and television broadcasts of Razorback games.

In 2010, ISP was acquired by IMG Worldwide, Inc., a global sports, entertainment, and media giant that became the nation's leading collegiate marketing and media company. ISP was combined with IMG's existing college sports group, representing the multimedia marketing interests of 80 colleges. Founded by the late sports-marketing pioneer Mark McCormack, IMG Worldwide is the world's largest sports talent and marketing agency and operates in more than 30 countries. The original star client was golfer Arnold Palmer.

IMG greatly expanded under the leadership of billionaire Ted Forstmann, one of the most influential figures in sports business. Forstmann, who died in 2011, had founded a private-equity firm and was one of those who created the leveraged buyout industry in the 1970s. He bought IMG in 2004 and greatly expanded it beyond a talent agency representing big names such as Roger Federer and Tiger Woods. Forstmann put the company's emphasis on collegiate licensing, European soccer, global television rights, and event management. In addition to its now dominant role in college sports media and marketing, IMG formed a joint venture in sports programming with CCTV, China's national television network. IMG also helped develop the Indian Premier Cricket League and owns media rights for sports leagues in a number of countries. Following Forstmann's death, Michael Dolan became the chief executive officer of IMG. Dolan had been a key figure in developing the company's global strategy, leading the expansion into China, India, and Brazil and into new business areas.

IMG began its move into college sports in 2007, buying the Collegiate Licensing Company (CLC) and then adding Host Communications, which handled broadcasting for a number of major college sports teams. Those two and later ISP became part of IMG College, which calls itself the nation's leading collegiate marketing, licensing, and media company, partnering with "some of the top brands in intercollegiate athletics." IMG College is headquartered in Winston-Salem, North Carolina.

IMG says it has the expertise, relationships, and properties to help clients reach their passionate supporters year-round, noting that the collegiate fan base nationally totals 172 million. At the time of IMG's acquisition of ISP, the Razorbacks' athletic director Jeff Long said, "We will work with the new company under our existing ISP agreement." He added that Arkansas would "maintain its relationship with the premier multimedia rights holder in intercollegiate athletics," which IMG clearly had become.

"This is going to give us more of a national platform to promote the Razorbacks. We'll be able to do things on a much larger scale and compete with Major League Baseball and the NFL," said Ryan Gribble, general manager of Razorback Sports Properties.

All Access, All the Time

When the University of Arkansas, KATV, and ARSN agreed to assign television and radio sports rights for the Razorbacks to ISP Sports in 2008 (which was acquired by IMG in 2010), that agreement came with a guaranteed total of $73 million to the university over 10 years. Under the agreement, KATV, which previously served as the official radio and television rights holder for Arkansas through ARSN, would remain the flagship television station of the new network. KATV general manager Dale Nicholson said, "We have enjoyed our four decade partnership with the University of Arkansas and are looking forward via our partnership with ISP as the continuing Home of the Razorbacks." ISP (and later IMG) also took responsibility for managing certain media rights that were once managed by the athletic department, including venue signage, printed materials such as game programs, the official athletic website, and expanded broadcast game packages. The UA athletic department created Razorback Sports Properties as its marketing and media unit.

As the multimedia rights holder, Razorback Sports Properties is responsible for all website, broadcast, corporate partnerships, and marketing of the university's athletics program, and is intended to bring a national presence to the marketing of Razorback sports. Razorback Sports Properties produces and markets radio and television broadcasts of Arkansas sports though the Razorback Sports Network from IMG, including all radio and TV play-by-play broadcasts, pay-per-view broadcasts, and radio head coaches' shows.

Broadcasting of sports events has not been without controversy, particularly as it has become more of a big business. But whether it was team officials and administrators who were concerned that broadcasts would hurt ticket sales, or Humble Oil making sure the Arkansas network stayed out of Texas, or Frank Broyles differing in opinion with KATV over who had the right to decide who would be the voice of the Razorbacks, or disputes about how much a particular conference or university would receive for television rights, there is a powerful interest among sports fans in broadcasts of the games.

With collegiate sports today, particularly football and basketball, having become big business—as has the media coverage—team followers and sports fans generally have much greater access to live coverage of sports events. The expansion in television coverage of intercollegiate athletics has been dramatic. Not too many years ago, only a few football games were carried live on television each week. For the 2011 football season, ABC and the various ESPN networks, all part of the Disney conglomerate, scheduled more than 250 games for TV coverage, with hundreds more carried on other national networks, regional cable networks, syndicated packages, and online.

The extensive coverage of Razorback sports was evident in 2010–11, with a school record 107 TV appearances by Razorback teams during the year. With the extensive SEC television package and partnerships with regional carriers such as Cox Sports Television, 12 different Razorback sports had at least one appearance on television. All football games and all SEC men's basketball games were televised. The Arkansas baseball team was on television 24 times in 2011 when not long ago almost the only way for college baseball teams to be seen on television was to qualify for the College World Series. The Razorback baseball team was also featured on a 30-minute ESPNU *All-Access* show, which provided a behind-the-scenes view of the home series with Mississippi State. For the first time, the spring Red-White football game was televised nationally on ESPN.

The 2011 BCS Sugar Bowl game with Arkansas matched against Ohio State earned a 9.5 TV rating, the third-highest college football rating for ESPN of all time, behind only the Auburn-Oregon national championship game and the 2011 Rose Bowl. Arkansas's home game with Alabama in September 2010 drew a 5.2 rating and 12 share for CBS, the network's best showing for a regular-season afternoon game since 2003.

For the 2011 football season, *Inside Razorback Football* was televised each Sunday night throughout the season on KATV and two Northwest Arkansas stations and at various times on Cox Cable systems. And the weekly *Bobby Petrino Live* radio show was carried by the Razorback Sports Network during the season, with Chuck Barrett serving as host. On football game days, the "Razorback Sports Network from IMG" provided not only live radio coverage of the games, but also a three-hour pre-game show and extensive post-game commentary and analysis.

KNWA in Northwest Arkansas and its sister TV station in Little Rock, KARK, feature what they call *Razorback Nation Sports*, with extensive reports on Razorback sports, anchored by Aaron Peters. In 2012, station officials said they were putting more resources into covering the Razorbacks than any other station. The stations proclaimed, "We are proud to be the Razorback Nation, the largest sports team in Arkansas." When the baseball Razorbacks made it to the 2012 College World Series in Omaha, KNWA had seven people from its Razorback Nation sports department covering the event. KNWA also hired veteran sportscaster Mike Irwin, who had been covering the Razorbacks since 1975 for another station and had established himself as an authoritative voice on Arkansas sports. The emphasis on the Razorback Nation brand by KNWA and KARK demonstrates the continuing high level of interest in Razorback sports. And KATV, the Little Rock station long identified with Razorback sports, boasts of "exclusive Razorback sports coverage" at "Hog Central."

Radio station KTTG, licensed to Mena and covering much of western Arkansas, emphasizes Razorback sports, along with ESPN programs and proclaims, "We know the Hogs." One of its popular shows is *SportsTalk with Bo*, featuring Bo Mattingly of Fayetteville, with Clay Henry and Dudley Dawson as regular commentators. The show is heard statewide on weekday afternoons on stations around the state and also carried on KXNW-TV in Northwest Arkansas. It boasts of being "the show of record for Hog fans" with the latest in Razorback sports. KTTG also carries a morning drive-time show with Derek Ruscin and Tommy Craft that focuses on Razorback sports. When Arkansas played in the 2012 Cotton Bowl, the program originated from Dallas.

Another Razorback-oriented station is "The Sports Hog," KHGG-FM, based in Waldron and Fort Smith. Grant Hall and Vernon Tarver, longtime print journalists, have a daily morning radio show in Fayetteville that focuses on the Razorbacks.

Satellite radio also carries Razorback games now, and SiriusXM Radio can be picked up by anyone who has the proper equipment, making it possible for far-away fans to tune in. That's just one of a number of alternative means for receiving reports and broadcasts of Razorback games. Hogwired.com and RazorVision would have seemed like futuristic fantasies in the early days of Razorback broadcasts but are now important elements in the array of opportunities for tuning in on the Razorbacks. RazorVision offers to subscribers live audio/video of many Razorback sports events. Ads for RazorVision subscriptions say that it will "give you all the video that Arkansas athletics has to offer—live sporting events, on-demand video, coaches and player interviews and much more 24 hours a day, at home or on the road on your laptop." And, of course, today there are blogs, websites, and message boards devoted to Razorback sports.

Meeting the Demand

The University of Arkansas's move to the SEC in the early 1990s positioned UA in a perfect spot when the significant increase in TV coverage of college sports developed in the following years and resulted in major increases in revenue for the SEC member schools. The huge contracts that the SEC has with CBS and ESPN would have been hard to imagine in the early days of Razorback broadcasts.

Following the 2012 season, *Forbes* magazine ranked Arkansas as the tenth most valuable team nationally in terms of financial value and revenue. Texas was ranked first, followed by Michigan and Notre Dame and then seven SEC teams, with LSU, Alabama, Florida, Auburn, and Tennessee ahead of Arkansas. The *Wall Street Journal*, reporting on an analysis of the "most valuable" college football teams for 2012, listed Arkansas as 14th nationally, valued at $332 million. The ranking was very similar to the *Forbes* list.

When Texas A&M and the University of Missouri joined the SEC in 2012, the larger TV revenue was a major factor, and the two new teams also brought additional large TV markets (Houston, Dallas, San Antonio, Austin for A&M; St. Louis and Kansas City for Missouri) to the SEC. In 2012, the SEC's revenue-sharing plan paid about $20.1 million to each member school (before A&M and Missouri officially became members), with money generated by television contracts for football and basketball, bowl games, the SEC championship game in football, the men's basketball tournament, and NCAA championships. During the 2011–12 academic year, Razorback athletic teams made 101 television appearances.

"The prices for collegiate TV rights are rising because the rabid fan bases for such sports are one of the few audiences TV programmers can count on to tune in for live broadcasts," the *Wall Street Journal* reported. In 2011, ESPN and the University of Texas agreed to establish the Longhorn Network, with ESPN paying about $11 million annually over 20 years, plus another $4 million to IMG. "There is a tremendous value in college sports," said Burke Magnus, ESPN's senior vice president for college sports programming. He said that the pageantry and the greater volume of programming compared with professional sports also help drive the demand for college sports.

ESPN's SEC Network

If there was any doubt about just how big the college sports business had become or about the close relationship between college sports and television, those doubts were erased in the spring of 2013 with the announcement of the creation of the SEC Network, operated by ESPN. Under a 20-year agreement effective August 2014, the SEC Network is expected to produce 1,000 live events each year, including 450 on the television network and 550 digitally. The network planned to carry 45 football games each season. The long-anticipated SEC Network deal was a 20-year extension of the existing ESPN contract, signed in 2008, which guaranteed the SEC $2.25 billion over 15 years. No specific financial terms were announced for the new deal, but it obviously involves a multi-billion-dollar agreement which will provide a substantial financial boost to UA and the other SEC member schools. Athletic Director Jeff Long said, "The network will provide unprecedented exposure for our program and our university while providing more opportunities for passionate Razorback fans all over the country to watch our student-athletes compete." "I think it's already been established that this network will be very successful in terms of distribution and development of potential revenue," SEC Commissioner Mike Slive said. "We wouldn't have done this if we didn't believe it was going to be in the long-term benefit of the league."

Meanwhile, the SEC's 15-year deal with CBS, signed in 2008, continues, with CBS retaining first choice for Saturday afternoon football in the marquee 2:30 p.m. time slot. CBS also has the rights to one prime-time evening game per season. The creation of the SEC Network means that ESPN will have yet another channel to present the conference games—beyond ESPN,

ESPN2, and ESPNU. The SEC Network will carry three football games a week, including one opposite CBS's. ESPN hopes to get 25 to 30 million subscribers in the 11-state SEC region, and millions more across the nation.

Conclusion: The Legacy

Although Razorback Sports Properties may now be a part of a far-flung global conglomerate and the announcer today may say, "This is the Razorback Sports Network from IMG College," its origin dates to Bob Cheyne's efforts in the early 1950s.

Despite the varied means and extensive opportunities for receiving Razorback games and news and information about Razorback sports today, it all got started with those early broadcasts by Bob Fulton and the creation of the distinctive Razorback network by Bob Cheyne at the urging of John Barnhill. And in subsequent years, the voices of the Razorbacks that became so familiar to thousands—Bud Campbell, Mike Nail, Paul Eells, and Chuck Barrett, all of whom became known around the state by their first names—and others involved with the broadcasts played a major role in creating and maintaining a passionate following for Razorback sports and becoming a central element in Arkansas life.

It is hard to find anyone in Arkansas or Razorback fans anywhere who do not have special memories of listening to or watching broadcasts of Razorback games, and broadcast coverage has been a major factor in building interest in and allegiance to Razorback sports. In a state full of rabid Razorback boosters, the broadcasts of Razorback games link all these people together. It truly is a network—not just a network of stations, but a network of Razorback fans. Indeed, not only do many Razorback rooters refer to the broadcasters on a first-name basis, they feel a personal connection with those who announce the games and cover the Razorbacks. This was evident in 2006 when longtime football play-by-play announcer Paul Eells died in an automobile accident, leading to a period of statewide mourning.

Razorback broadcasts have grown in scope over the decades from a small-scale beginning on radio to a large radio network and extensive television and online coverage. Even today, with most Razorback games available on television, many fans watching prefer to turn down the volume of the TV broadcast and listen to the voice of the Razorbacks.

Index

ABC, 40, 41, 52, 62, 65, 69, 71, 94, 104, 127

Abilene Christian College, 20

Adams, Glen, 120

Adams, Joe, 131

Aikman, Troy, 62

Alabama (University of), 23, 32, 72, 107, 146

Alexander, Connie, 18

Allen, Mel, 38, 39

Allen, Nate, 38, 101, 120

Alworth, Lance, 70

American Football League (AFL), 40

Anderson, Jamaal, 96

Anderson, Mike, 131, 136. *See also Full-Court Press; Mike'd Up.*

Arkadelphia, Arkansas, 55, 72

Arkansas Alumni Association, 41

Arkansas Business, 113

Arkansas congressional delegation, 54

Arkansas Democrat, 36

Arkansas Democrat-Gazette, 37, 73, 81, 83, 84, 95, 117

Arkansas Educational Television Network (AETN), 98

Arkansas Gazette, 24, 34, 36, 39, 61, 71

Arkansas Intercollegiate Conference (AIC), 29, 55

Arkansas Radio Network (ARN), 107

Arkansas Razorback Sports Network (ARSN), 12, 13, 33, 71, 81, 107, 111, 113, 121, 125. *See also* Razorback network.

"Arkansas Scouting Report," 61

Arkansas Sports Hall of Fame, 130

Arkansas Sportswriters and Sportscasters Hall of Fame, 53

Arkansas State Teachers College, 72

Arkansas State University, 111

Arkansas Tech, 55

Arkansas Times, 123

Arkansas Travelers, 30, 53, 133, 134

(Note: Listing of Arkansas vs. opponents refers to football unless otherwise indicated.)

Arkansas vs. Alabama, 32, 96, 143

Arkansas vs. Auburn, 96

Arkansas vs. Baylor (basketball), 59; (baseball), 116

Arkansas vs. Duke (basketball), 95, 99

Arkansas vs. Georgia, 41, 73,

Arkansas vs. Georgia Tech, 34

Arkansas vs. Houston (basketball), 100

Arkansas vs. Kentucky, 81, 88; (basketball), 100

Arkansas vs. Louisiana–Monroe, 15

Arkansas vs. Louisville (basketball), 104

Arkansas vs. LSU, 25, 55, 80, 84, 87, 97, 106, 118, 126, 134

Arkansas vs. Miami, 62

Arkansas vs. Mississippi (Ole Miss), 34, 35, 36, 37 38, 43, 47, 80, 81, 88, 124; (basketball), 101

Arkansas vs. Mississippi State (basketball) 134, (baseball), 143

Arkansas vs. Missouri, 104

Arkansas vs. Missouri State, 131

Arkansas vs. North Carolina (basketball), 100, 101

Arkansas vs. Ohio State, 143
Arkansas vs. Oklahoma, 75, 106
Arkansas vs. Rice, 58, 59
Arkansas vs. San Diego State
    (baseball), 133
Arkansas vs. South Carolina, 32, 96,
    127
Arkansas vs. Southern Methodist
    University (SMU), 38;
    (basketball), 100
Arkansas vs. Tennessee, 80, 85, 87,
    96, 97, 123; (basketball), 100
Arkansas vs. Texas, 29, 36, 43, 54,
    55, 62, 67-69, 71, 75, 80, 88,
    104, 128, 138; (basketball), 100
Arkansas vs. Texas Christian
    University (TCU), 34, 72
Arkansas vs. Texas Tech, 62
Arkansas vs. Tulsa, 69
Arkansas vs. University of
    California, Los Angeles
    (UCLA), 62
Arkansas vs. University of Nevada–
    Las Vegas (UNLV),
    (basketball), 100
Arkansas vs. University of Southern
    California, 71, 85, 96
Arkansas vs. Vanderbilt, 106
Arkansas vs. Virginia (baseball), 116
Arkansas vs. Wichita (freshmen), 58
Arkansas vs. Wichita State
    (baseball), 115
Arledge, Roone, 41, 65, 68
Associated Press, 70
Associated Press poll, 34, 38
Atlanta, Georgia, 83
Atlanta Braves, 83
Atlanta Hawks, 101
Auburn University, 121, 146
Austin, Texas, 52, 54, 55, 61, 88, 146
Bagley, Quinton, 120

Bahn, Chris, 117
Bailey, Jim, 36, 53
Balentine, Charles, 101
Barnes, Steve, 83
Barnhill, John, 12, 19, 20, 23, 25,
    26, 40, 41, 43, 149
Barnhill Arena, 73, 100
Barrett, Chuck, 13, 14, 87, 105, 106,
    109, 111, 113–129, 132–137,
    143, 149
Barton, Dan, 31
baseball broadcasts (Razorbacks),
    13, 113, 115–118, 120–122,
    129, 132, 134
Baton Rouge, 123
Baum Stadium, 115, 116
Baylor University, 107
Bazzel, David, 130
Beadle, Liz, 81
Beck, Cory, 101
Benson, Buddy Bob, 35–38, 47
Bentonville, 56
Bielema, Bret, 135, 136
Birmingham, Alabama, 19
Birmingham, DeCori, 87
Blattner, Buddy, 97
Bobby Petrino Live, 135, 143
Booras, Tommy, 73, 74, 79, 82, 97
Booty, John David, 96
Boston Red Sox, 38
Brackett, Deke, 26
Bradford, Eddie, 37
Bradley, Pat, 130
Brandt, Barry, 83
Bret Bielema Show, 136
Brewer, Jim, 70
Brewer, Ron, 73
Brewer, Ronnie, 101
Brittenum, Jon, 55, 70
Brooklyn Dodgers, 38
Brooks, Bud, 37

Broyles, Frank, 12, 51–53, 57, 60-63, 67–69, 73, 74, 80, 85, 90, 95, 98, 99, 101, 102, 106, 111–114, 127, 137, 142. *See also Frank Broyles Show.*
Brown, Tony, 101
Bryant, Paul "Bear," 23
Buck, Jack, 104, 118, 125
Bud Walton Arena, 136
Buffalo Bills, 128
Burton, Billie J., 82
Bush, George H. W., 68
Cadillac, 42, 43
Cain, Scott, 83, 84
Calcagni, Ron, 106
Campbell, Claude "Bud," 53, 54, 57, 60–65, 69, 70, 72, 73, 77, 83, 98, 105, 106, 115, 119, 124, 149
Campbell, Claude "Bud," death of, 69, 71
Campbell, Leon "Muscles," 19, 25
Canada, Eugene "Bud," 25
Caray, Harry, 104, 125
Carnegie (Tech) Mellon University, 33
Carpenter, Ched, 86
Carpenter, Preston, 35, 36, 37, 38, 47
Carver, Bob, 105, 106
Catfish Hole, 135
Cawood, Dave, 72
CBS, 17, 27, 28, 38, 104, 126, 129, 130, 143, 147, 148
CBS contract with SEC, 139, 145, 147
CCTV (China Central Television), 140
Celebrate Arkansas, 12
Central Arkansas, 112, 113, 134
Cedar Rapids, Iowa, 79
Charlotte Bobcats, 75
Charlotte Hornets, 75

Charlotte, North Carolina, 95
Chesser, Alec, 18
Cheyne, Bob, 11, 15, 16, 20-28, 32, 33, 42, 45, 46, 50-52, 54, 56-59, 64, 70, 97, 99, 104, 124, 149
Cheyne, Jennie, 22, 51, 60
Chicago, Illinois, 25
Chicago Bears, 130
Chicago Bulls, 129
Chicago Cubs (broadcasts), 104, 125
Cincinnati Reds, 41
Claridge Hotel, Memphis, 59
Clarksville, Arkansas, 17, 28, 120
Clarksville High School Panthers, 120
Cleveland Browns, 37
Cobbs, Cedric, 88
Coffey, Charlie, 61, 65
College World Series, 14, 115, 122, 143, 144
College (University) of the Ozarks, 17, 28
Collegiate Licensing Company, 140
Colorado Rockies, 41
Columbia, Missouri, 51
Columbia, South Carolina, 29
Columbia Reds, 29
Comcast Sports, 132
Connors, Bill, 104
Conway High School Wampus Cats, 71
Conway, Arkansas, 114
Cook, Beano, 68
Cotton Bowl, 14, 19, 25, 33, 36, 38, 39, 55, 56, 62, 80, 104, 118, 130, 144
Cotton States League, 31
Cox Sports Television, 136, 137, 143
Cox, Zack, 116
Craft, Tommy, 81
Crawford, London, 126
Crockett, Bobby, 55

Crump Stadium, 20
Dallas, Texas, 40, 100, 101, 144, 146
Dallas Cowboys, 85
Dallas-Fort Worth Spurs, 40
Dallas Texans, 40, 41
Daugherty, Brad, 101
Davis, Knile, 126
Dawson, Dudley, 144
Day, Todd, 101
Dean, Dizzy, 31
DeBriyn, Norm, 122
Delph, Marvin, 73
Demaree Media, 121
Denver Nuggets, 131
De Queen, Arkansas, 37
Dick, Casey, 124, 126
Dicus, Chuck, 106
Disney conglomerate, 142
Dixie Bowl, 19
Dodd, Bobby, 51, 52
Dokes, James, 105
Dolan, Michael, 140
Dottley, John "Kayo," 23
Douglas, Otis, 44
Dover, Arkansas, 82
Drive Time Sports, 130
Dunlap, J. E., 85
Dykes, Jimmy, 84, 131, 132
East Liverpool, Ohio, 74
Eells, Paul, 15, 53, 69, 72, 77, 79,
    81- 96, 103, 104, 106, 107, 115,
    119, 123-125, 127, 131, 137,
    149, 150. See also "Paul's Calls."
Eells, Paul, death of, 69, 82–86, 95,
    96, 108, 150
Eibner, Brett, 116
Eddins, Blake, 125, 132
Elder, Jim, 30, 31, 53, 104, 105, 115
"1190 'The Fan,'" Fayetteville, 86
El Dorado, Arkansas, 22
Elliott, Marcus, 130

Elson, Phil, 133
Emmy awards, 67
ESPN networks, 14, 75, 118, 125,
    131, 132, 137, 139, 142–144,
    146–148
ESPN, agreement with SEC, 139,
    145, 147, 148
Esso (Standard Oil), 18
European soccer, 140
Evatt, Dan, 116
Exxon (Standard Oil), 18
Fahr, Rick, 14, 15
Farrell, Robert, 71
Fayetteville, 22, 24, 28, 29, 58, 67,
    68, 72, 74, 82, 86, 87, 96, 97,
    98, 102, 107, 111–114, 118,
    132, 135, 145
Fayetteville High, 33
Federer, Roger, 140
Ferguson, Joe, 106, 121, 128, 129
Fleming, Bill, 68
Florida, University of, 146
Fogg, Bill, 22
Foley, Larry, 70
Football Writers Association, 52, 58
Forbes magazine, 145, 146
Ford, Danny, 121–123, 129
Fordyce, Arkansas, 23
Forrest City, Arkansas, 22, 26, 36
Forstmann, Ted, 140
Fort Smith, 13, 39, 41, 42, 81, 98,
    99, 120, 132
Fox network, 130
Fox Sports Net, 132
Fox Sports South/Southwest, 136,
    137
Frank Broyles Show, 52, 53, 60, 61,
    62, 63, 71
Frank Broyles Field, 127
Frei, Terry, 67
Freeze, Jack, 39, 41

Fulbright, J. William, 68
Full-Court Press, 136
Fulton, Bob, 17, 27, 28, 30, 31, 32, 149
Fulton, Dody, 28
Game of the Week, 97, 118
Georgia Tech, 51
Georgia, University of, 83, 124
Gowdy, Curt, 38
Graham, Billy, 68
Grand Ole Opry, 80
Grange, Red, 39
"Great Shootout" of 1969, 41, 62, 67, 68, 69. *See also* Arkansas vs. Texas.
Green Bay Packers, 127, 138
Greenville, South Carolina, 32
Gribble, Ryan, 141
Grovey, Quinn, 103, 121, 128, 129
Hall, Grant, 33, 71, 81, 102, 145
Hamilton, Cobi, 126
Hammerschmidt, John Paul, 68
Hampton, Dan, 130
Hanner, Dave "Hawg," 138
Harris, E. Lynn, 70
Harris, Fred, 68
Harris, Jim, 124
Harrison Daily Times, 85
Hartman High, 28
Hastings, Scott, 131
Hatfield, Ken, 21, 55, 74
Hawgs Illustrated, 13, 15, 115, 121
Heath, Stan, 99, 132
Heber Springs, 28
Heck, Howell, 72
Helena, Arkansas, 24
Hendrix College, 71
Henry, Clay, 15, 115, 121, 144
Henry, Orville, 24, 26, 34, 36, 53, 61, 65, 71, 104, 105, 115, 123
Heverling, Rob, 83

Hickman, Herman, 39
Hillis, Peyton, 96
Hogwired.com, 145
Holtz, Lou, 61, 74, 75, 80, 93, 137. *See also Lou Holtz Show.*
Hornell, New York, 29
Horns, Hogs, & Nixon Coming, 67
Host Communications, 18, 140
Hot Springs, 25
Hot Springs Bathers, 31
Hot Springs *Sentinel-Record*, 55
Houston, Texas, 58, 146
Houston, Chris, 96
Houston College Classic, 134
Houston, University of, 18
Houston Nutt Show, 96, 97, 123
Huckabee, Mike, 85
Hughes, Ryan, 15
Humble Oil and Refining Co., 17, 18, 20, 21, 50, 142
Humble broadcasts, 17, 18, 20, 48, 50, 56, 57
Hunt, Lamar, 40
IMG/IMG College, 16, 107, 135,140–142, 146, 149
IMG Worldwide, Inc., 140
India Premier Cricket League, 140
Ingalls, Wallie, 24, 32, 33, 39, 50
Ingram, Cecil "Hootie," 61, 65
Inman, Scott, 83, 111, 113-115, 131, 132
Inside Razorback Athletics, 99, 134
Inside Razorback Football with Bobby Petrino, 137, 138
Iowa, 79
Iowa, University of, 79, 107
ISDN (Integrated Services Digital Network), 106, 107
ISP Sports, 139–141
Irwin, Mike, 136
Jackson, Keith (ABC), 52, 104, 127

Jackson, Keith (Arkansas network),
    52, 53, 84, 106, 126, 127, 128
Jackson, Keith, Jr., 127
James, Bruce, 130
John Pelphrey Live, 136
Johnson, Jimmy, 130
Johnson, Bill, 71, 72
Johnson, Joe, 101
Johnson, Mervin, 61, 65
Johnson, Robert, 88
Jonesboro, Arkansas, 111, 132
Jones, Charlie, 39, 40, 41, 42
Jones, Felix, 96, 97
Jones, Harry "Light Horse," 70
Jones, Jerry, 85
Jones, Matt (player), 84, 87, 130
Jones, Matt (writer), 13
Joplin, Missouri, 51, 99
Jordan, Michael, 101
Justus, John, 134
KAAY, Little Rock, 56, 103
Kansas, 58
Kansas, University of, 43
Kansas City, Missouri, 146
Kansas City Chiefs, 40
Kansas State, 14
KAGH, Crossett, 118
KAMD, Camden, 22
KARN, Little Rock, 121
KARK-TV, Little Rock, 52, 53, 60,
    72, 73, 74, 144
KARV, Russellville, 120
KATV, Little Rock, 14, 52, 53, 60,
    61, 63, 65, 69, 72–75, 79, 80, 82,
    83, 91–94, 98, 105, 107, 111,
    113, 123, 131, 137, 141–144
KDRS, Paragould, 22
Kellams, Kyle, 133, 134
Kemp, Kelly, 12
Kentucky, University of, 131
KFAY, Fayetteville, 120, 121

KFFA, Helena, 13, 22, 118
KFPW, Fort Smith, 39
KFSA, Fort Smith, 18, 48
KFSM-TV , Fort Smith, 98
KFTA, Northwest Arkansas, 137
KGRH, Fayetteville, 18, 33, 50
KHBS-KHOG (40/29), 108
KHGG-FM, Waldron-Fort Smith
    ("The Sports Hog"), 145
King, Cyd, 95, 97
King, Harry, 11, 31, 53, 70, 71, 72,
    84, 105, 115
Kissinger, Henry, 68
KLCN, Blytheville, 22
Kleine, Joe, 101, 129
KLRA, Little Rock, 17, 28, 49
KMAG, Fort Smith, 120
KNOE-TV, Monroe, Louisiana, 72,
    73
Knoxville, Tennessee, 17, 43
KNWA, Fayetteville, 100, 114, 137,
    144
KTVE-TV, El Dorado, 73
KTHV, Little Rock, 70
KTTG, western Arkansas, 144
KWEM, West Memphis, 17
KWTK, Oklahoma City, 99
KXJK, Forrest City, 22
KXLR, North Little Rock, 17, 29
KXNW-TV, Northwest Arkansas,
    144
Lang, Andrew, 101
Larson, Don, 97
Las Vegas Invitational Basketball
    Tournament, 134
Learfield Sports, 107
Lemke Department of Journalism,
    26, 135
Lemke, Walter J., 26
Lexington, Kentucky, 18, 88
Life magazine, 39

Lindsey, Harold "Rip," 59
Lindsey, Jim, 21, 36
Little Rock, 13, 19, 21, 28–30, 52, 58, 59, 69-71, 80-83, 104, 107, 111–114, 121, 126–128, 130, 144
Little Rock (Central) High School, 28, 61
Log Cabin Democrat (Conway), 14, 114, 124
London, England, 27
Long, Jeff, 112, 113, 133, 141
Longhorn Network, 146
Lonoke, Arkansas, 67
Lorenzen, Jared, 88
Los Angeles, 74
Los Angeles Chargers, 41
Los Angeles Dodgers, 38, 117
Louie's Bar and Grill, 136
Louisiana, 58
Lou Holtz Show, 93
Louisiana State University (LSU), 15, 23
Lucas, Anthony, 85, 87, 103
Luigs, Jonathan, 96
Madden, John, 130
Magnus, Burke, 146
Major League Baseball, 11, 118, 125, 141
Mallett, Ryan, 126
Manning, Eli, 88
Markham Street, 20
Matthews, Wilson, 61, 65
Mattingly, Bo, 144
Mayberry, Lee, 101, 103
Master's golf tournament, 130
McClellan, John, 68
McCollum, David, 114, 124
McConnell, Jerry, 53
McCormack, Mark, 140
McDonald's, 84
McFadden, Darren, 88, 96

McGehee, Arkansas 23
McKinney, Russell, 21-22, 23
Memphis Commercial Appeal, 37
Memphis, Tennessee, 20, 34, 59, 120
Mercer, Bill, 40
message boards, 124
Miami Dolphins, 127
Miami Heat, 75
Michigan, University of, 146
Mike'd Up, 136
Miller, Oliver, 101
Miller, Scott, 120
Minnesota, University of, 51, 137
Minute Maid Park, 134
"Miracle on Markham," 80, 87, 126
Mississippi, University of (Ole Miss), 23, 35, 123
Missouri, 58
Missouri, University of, 51, 107, 146
Mitchell, Jack, 43, 51
Moncrief, Sidney, 73, 101, 103
"Monday Night Football," 67
Montgomery, Alabama, 72
Montgomery, Bill, 106
Mooney, George, 17
Moore, Billy, 70
"Most Valuable" college football teams, 146
Mountain Inn, 29
Munoz, Christina, 83
Munson, Larry, 83, 124
Mutual Broadcasting System, 18, 27, 29, 31
Mutual Game of the Day, 27, 31, 32
Nail, Mike, 12, 76, 95–104, 107, 108, 117, 120, 121, 124, 127, 129, 132, 133, 149
Nantz, Jim, 104
Nashville, Tennessee, 79, 83
National Basketball Association (NBA), 75, 129, 131

National Football League (NFL),
    29, 37, 40, 52, 79, 127–130,
    138, 141
National Invitational Tournament
    (NIT), 99
NBC, 38, 39, 40, 41, 55, 75, 114, 130
NCAA baseball regionals/super-
    regionals, 115, 116, 125
NCAA basketball tournament, 38,
    73, 82, 99, 100, 103, 104, 146
Arkansas National Champions, 91,
    92, 96, 99, 100, 103. 136. See
    also 1994 National Champions.
"NCAA Pre-Game Show," 61
Nelson, Lindsey, 39, 55
Nessler, Brad, 132
New Mexico, 56
New Orleans, Louisiana, 32
New York Giants, 129
New York Mets, 39
New York Times, 75
New York Yankees, 38, 97
Nicholson, Dale, 111, 113, 114, 141
1954 football season, 34-39, 42, 47
1964 national champions (football),
    52, 54, 55
1977 football season, 75
1994 national champions
    (basketball), 91, 92, 94, 96, 99–
    101, 103, 136
Nixon, Richard, 67, 68, 69
Nolan Richardson Show, 89, 91
Northwest Arkansas, 99, 102, 108,
    111, 144
Northwest Arkansas Times, 25, 26
Notre Dame, University of, 137
Nutt, Houston, 82, 85, 97, 123, 124.
    See also Houston Nutt Show.
Nutt, Houston, "Arkansan of the
    Year," 123
"Oh my," 80, 84, 87

Oklahoma, 58, 68, 103
Oklahoma State University, 103, 131
Oklahoma, University of, 43, 52, 68,
    107, 127, 128
Olympics, 19, 41, 65, 101, 129
Omaha, Nebraska, 116, 122
Orange Bowl, 75, 106
Orlando, Florida, 97
Ouachita Baptist University, 37
Oxford, Mississippi, 88, 124
Palmer, Arnold, 140
"Passing-est teams of 1936–37," 35
"Paul's Calls," 86–88
Pelphrey, John, 99, 136
Perkins, Sam, 101
Peters, Aaron, 144
Petrino, Bobby, 135, 137, 138
Petty, Jermaine, 88
Philadelphia, 17
Philadelphia Eagles, 29, 30, 31, 127
Pierce, Mark, 88
Pine Bluff, Arkansas, 84, 100, 101
Pine Bluff Convention Center, 100,
    101
Poinsettia Basketball Classic, 32
Polikoff, Rich, 117, 133
Poplar Bluff, Missouri, 60
"Powder River Play," 35
Presbyterian Church, 28
Pro Football Hall of Fame, 41, 130
Pro Football Weekly, 130
Pueblo, Colorado, 29
Pulaski Heights Junior High, 28
Quigley Stadium, 19, 29
Rainwater, Randy, 81, 103
Rand, Ted, 22
Razorback Club, 67
Razorback Baseball with Dave Van
    Horn, 136
Razorback Football with John L.
    Smith, 135

Razorback Nation, 123
Razorback Nation Sports, 144
Razorback (U of A) network, 11–13,
    16, 19–23, 27, 32, 33, 38, 42,
    45, 46, 50, 52, 54–58, 60, 64,
    69–75, 80–82, 84, 87, 88, 95–
    97, 99–107, 110, 111, 113–122,
    124–132, 136, 142, 145, 149,
    150. *See also* Arkansas
    Razorback Sports Network.
"Razorback Radio Rooters," 49
"Razorback Roundup," 57, 58, 64
Razorback Sports Properties, 139,
    141, 142, 149
Razorback Stadium, 19, 20, 58, 69,
    111, 127
Razorback yearbook, 37
RazorVision, 135, 137, 145
RazorVision Academy, 135
Reagan, Ronald, 30
re-creation broadcasts, 29, 30, 31,
    40, 53–54
recruiting, 20, 23, 26
Red-White game, 33, 57, 136, 143
Reed, U. S., 104
Reese, Pee Wee, 97
Reynolds Razorback Stadium, 127.
    See also Razorback Stadium.
Richardson, Nolan, 84, 89, 91, 132,
    136. *See also Nolan Richardson
    Show*.
Robertson, Alvin, 101
Rockefeller, Winthrop, 68
Rogers, Bill, 132
Roosevelt, Franklin Delano, 19
Rose Bowl, 38
Royal, Darrell, 61, 67
"Running Razorbacks," 98
Ruscin, Derek, 144
Russellville, 21, 55, 82
St. Louis, Missouri, 146

St. Louis Cardinals (broadcasts), 31,
    104, 118, 125
San Antonio, 146
San Antonio Spurs, 75
San Francisco Giants, 39
Sassy's Red House, 136
Schaeffer, Rick, 14, 87, 102–107,
    117, 118, 122, 129
Schenkel, Chris, 68, 71
Schoonover, Wear, 26–27
Scoreboard Show, 58, 64, 115
Scott, Clyde ("Smackover"), 19, 25,
    27, 29, 33
Scully, Vince, 38, 117
SEC Network, 132, 139, 147, 148
Shaw, Cliff, 54
Shoats (UA freshman team), 58
Shreveport, Louisiana, 60
single-wing formation, 35
SiriusXM Radio, 145
Slive, Mike, 147
Smith, Billy Ray, Jr., 103, 106
Smith, Sam, 75, 79, 104
South Atlantic (Sally) League, 29
South Carolina, University of, 27,
    29, 32, 137
South Dakota, 56
Southeastern Conference (SEC), 17,
    32, 35, 38, 50, 83, 92, 96, 100,
    112, 121, 132, 133, 139, 145–
    147
Southwest Conference (SWC), 17–
    20, 25, 32, 36, 73, 100, 107
Southwest Conference Radio
    Network, 76
Southwestern Bell, 21
"Southwest Football Roundup," 61
Southwest-Times Record, Fort Smith,
    48
SportingLifeArkansas.com, 124
Sports Illustrated, 35

Sports-talk radio, 13, 81, 102, 113, 121, 130, 131

Sports Talk With Bo, 144

Sports Rap, 113, 121

Springdale, Arkansas, 22

"stadium debate," 111–113

Star City, Arkansas, 84

Steel, Bob, 123

Stephens Media, 70

Stewart, Dwight, 101

Stewart, Walter, 37

Stoerner, Clint, 85, 87

Stonebridge Meadows Golf Club, 82

Stuttgart, Arkansas, 111

Stumpe, Joe, 73

Sudbury, Harold, 22

Sugar Bowl, 32, 33, 41, 73, 126, 143

Sugg, Alan, 24

Suggs, Colby, 116

Sullivan, Steve, 82, 83

Summerall, Pat, 53, 129, 130, 138

Super Bowl, 130

Sutton, Eddie, 73, 80, 99, 130, 131

Switzer, Barry, 21, 130

Tarver, Vernon, 145

Taylor, Brad, 103

Tennessee, 58

Tennessee Titans, 79

Tennessee, University of, 39, 43

television, 13, 14, 33, 39, 41, 50, 54, 57, 61–65, 69, 73–75, 80, 91, 92, 98, 99, 102, 104, 105, 113, 114, 115, 118, 123, 126, 129–132, 135–139, 141–148, 150

Texarkana, Arkansas, 22, 40, 136

Texas A&M University, 146

Texas League, 134

Texas Tech, 18

Texas, University of, 20, 36, 61, 146

Thanksgiving (1997), 122, 123

Thurman, Scotty, 99, 101, 103

Tips, Kern, 18

Tonight Show (NBC), 74

"Touchdown Arkansas!," 80, 84, 85, 87, 125, 126

Toops, Brady, 115, 117

track and field, 33

Trainor, Kevin, 85, 134

Tucker, Ray, 132

Tulsa, Oklahoma, 29

Tulsa World, 104

Turner, Matt, 100

"25 Little Pigs," 34

"22 Straight," 70

2006 football season, 96

United Press International poll, 71

United Service Organization (USO), 25

United States Army, 37

United States Open tennis, 130

University of Arkansas Sports Hall of Fame, 130

University of Central Arkansas (UCA), 72

University of Louisiana–Monroe (Northeast Louisiana), 15, 73

Vanderbilt University, 79, 83

Van Eman, Lanny, 98

Van Horn, Dave, 122, 136, 137

Vertical Arkansas, 15

Villa Capri Motel, 62

Waco, Texas, 59, 116

Walker, Darrell, 101

Walker, George, 35, 54, 57, 64

Wall Street Journal, 146

Warmath, Murray, 51

War Memorial Stadium, 19, 20, 21, 29, 36, 62, 111

War Memorial Stadium Commission, 112

Warren, Arkansas, 26

Washington, DC, 54

WBAP-TV, Fort Worth, 34
Western Union, 31, 56
West Memphis, Arkansas, 29
White House, 30
"Whoa, Nellie!," 127
Wide World of Sports, 41, 67
Wiley, Ted, 26
William and Mary, 19
Williamson, Corliss, 101
Wimbledon tennis, 41
WIND, Chicago, 60
Wilkinson, Bud, 68
Wisener, Bob, 55
WMC, Memphis, 59
women's sports (Arkansas), 134, 135
Woodman, Dave, 71, 72, 73, 74, 75,
     76, 104
Woods, Tiger, 140
World Cup soccer, 41
World Series, 97
World War II, 25, 27
Works Progress Administration
     (WPA), 19
Wright, Jim, 68
WSM-TV, Nashville, 79, 80, 83
Wyatt, Bowden, 34, 42, 43
Wyoming, 35
Wyoming, University of, 35, 38
Zeigler, Doug, 88

About the Authors

Hoyt Purvis has taught at the University of Arkansas since 1982, teaching courses in journalism, international relations, and political science. He established the first sports journalism course at the University in 1984 and taught it for 25 years. He is a native of Jonesboro, Arkansas.

Stanley Sharp of Booneville, Arkansas, has followed Razorback sports throughout his life and received a master's degree in journalism from the University of Arkansas in 2009.

CPSIA information can be obtained
at www.ICGtesting.com
Printed in the USA
JSHW050541210722
28307JS00002B/141

9 781935 106623